Pyren

Roger Büdeler

Pyrenees 2

French Central Pyrenees:
Arrens to Seix

50 selected valley and high mountain walks
in the French Central Pyrenees

With 2 black and white and 78 colour photos,
50 small walking maps to a scale of 1:25,000, 1:50,000 and 1:75,000
and 2 contextualising maps to a scale of 1:650,000 and 1:900,000

ROTHER · MUNICH

Front cover: Cirque de Gavarnie

Frontispiece (page 2):
symbol of the Hautes Pyrénées: Brèche de Roland (Walk 13)

All photos by the author except for those on pages 50 and 87
by Lucien Briet (by kind consent of the Musée Pyrénéen)

Cartography:
walking maps to a scale of 1:25,000 / 1:50,000 / 1:75,000:
Kartografie Christian Rolle, Holzkirchen
contextualising maps to a scale of 1:650,000 / 1:900,000
© Freytag & Berndt, Vienna

Translation:
Gill Round

1st edition 2004
© Bergverlag Rother GmbH, Munich

ISBN 3-7633-4826-3

Distributed in Great Britain by Cordee, 3a De Montfort Street, Leicester
Great Britain LE1 7HD, www.cordee.co.uk

ROTHER WALKING GUIDES

Algarve · Andalusia South · Azores · Bernese Oberland East · Corsica · Côte d'Azur ·
Crete East · Crete West · Cyprus · Gomera · Gran Canaria · Iceland · La Palma · Madeira · Mallorca ·
Mont Blanc · Norway South · Provence · Pyrenees 1, 2, 3 · Sardinia · Sicily · High Tatra · Tenerife ·
Tuscany North · Valais East · Valais West · Vanoise · Around the Zugspitze

**Dear mountain lovers! We would be happy to hear your opinion
and suggestions for amendment to this Rother walking guide.**

BERGVERLAG ROTHER · Munich
**D-85521 Ottobrunn · Haidgraben 3 · Tel. (089) 608669-0, Fax -69
Internet www.rother.de · E-mail bergverlag@rother.de**

Foreword

Volume 2 of the Pyrenees series by Rother publishing covers the French Central Pyrenees between Val d'Azun in the west and Vallée d'Ustou in the east. It can be seen as a companion to volume 1, the Spanish Central Pyrenees. Both of these mountain regions share much of their border along the central main ridge and with their well-known national parks and nature reserves, are amongst the most attractive hiking areas in the whole of the Pyrenean chain.

There is no other more famous destination in the French Central Pyrenees than the Cirque de Gavarnie. It is the symbol of the Parque National des Pyrénées and for a long time this natural icon has been, quite simply, synonymous with the Pyrenees. Even Kurt Tucholsky poked fun a little at this huge spectacle and spoke disrespectfully of the 'national myth' which thousands of visitors paid homage to by going to see the huge valley basin. The appeal of this natural spectacle today continues and since it has been incorporated into the Unesco list of cultural heritage together with the neighbouring Cirques d'Estaubé and Troumouse, the Cirque de Gavarnie has become a world famous attraction way beyond the mountain hiking fraternity. Just as unrelenting is the summer rush of visitors to the superb amphitheatre with its magnificently shaped limestone rocks and plummeting waterfalls.

Surprisingly, however, you can still enjoy a walk round a Cirque de Gavarnie in relative peace. This is especially true of the other hiking areas in the French Central Pyrenees whose scenic diversity and contrasts are no less fascinating and impressive. Deep green pastures, enchanting forests, thundering waterfalls, meadows strewn with flowers, delightful mountain lakes, huge valley basins and statuesque peaks come together in a captivating region with powerful images and experiences at every turn. Not only Gavarnie, but also Balaitous, Vignemale, Marcadau, Néouvielle, Mont Valier or the mountains around the Luchon area are high on the list for many mountain hikers, not least because of the wealth of enjoyable hikes at alpine altitudes and in secluded valleys, to delightful lakes or along a line of gently rolling hills. Even the 'summits' and crests of the moderately high foothills frequently offer stunning views of the high alpine Pyrenees.

The walks contained in this guide represent a selection only of the countless hiking trails. They are meant to give mountain lovers an overview and point of reference as they become acquainted with the area, or explore it more intensively, and to make it possible to discover the scenic richness of the French Central Pyrenees in whatever way they choose. It only remains for me to wish you many enjoyable days in the French Central Pyrenees!

Spring 2004   Roger Büdeler

Contents

Vallée d'Aure and Néouvielle

Bagnères-de-Luchon

Couserans

Tourist tips

Using the guide

The hiking region of the French Central Pyrenees is subdivided into several main valleys. It starts in the west with Val'Azun and stretches eastwards to the Vallée d'Ustou and in between them lie the Vallées de Cauterets, Gavarnie, d'Aure and de la Pique. The Parc National des Pyrénées and the Néouvielle and Mont Valier national parks are specially protected mountain regions.

At the beginning of each individual walk there is an information section indicating the most important features of the walk, including suggestions for accommodation and places to eat and some helpful tips when planning the route. Where appropriate there are also ideas for extending or linking the walks and for alternative routes. A short introduction characterizes the walk and points out the interesting details. The walk description itself is kept as concise as possible, but includes a clear description of the route, the line of which is also marked on the small colour walking map. Listed in the index are all the walk destinations and relevant towns or villages, valleys and regions, as well as the huts. A contextualising map shows the location of the all the walks.

Grades

Almost all the hiking paths in this guide are well constructed and maintained. You will frequently find signposts at the start of each walk and en route at most of the crucial forks. As a rule, the details given about walking times are only a guide and of course apply under normal conditions. GR paths (Grande Randonnée) together with their alternatives are waymarked in white and red, next to which you will find the corresponding regional colour marking and sometimes numbers as well. Only very few stretches in this guide go over rough or unclear ground, but in this case they are waymarked with cairns.

On the French side of the Pyrenees in particular, you should take into account the possibility of sudden changes in the weather and rising fog. Also, one also shouldn't underestimate the strength of the sun's rays on the 'cooler' north side of the mountain range, especially on high-level routes and on walks where there is no shade. An adequate supply of water is essential on every walk and can be replenished at most refuges.

The colour numbering of the hiking tours stand for the various grades at the walker's disposal. They have the following meaning:

BLUE

Easy and danger-free walk on obvious paths and tracks. The walks are of limited length and are usually only moderately steep; there are greater variations in height on longer walks.

RED

Moderately difficult routes demand a greater degree of energy and fitness due to their length as well as the steeper and more persistent gradients. Paths waymarked in red can be narrow and can include slightly exposed sections and some short bits of scrambling. Special mention of these sections is made in the text. Hiking experience in the mountains as well as sure-footedness and a good sense of direction are essential.

BLACK

These difficult and long walks in the high mountains should only be undertaken by experienced and fit mountain hikers. Together with big variations in height, strenuous sections of steep ascent and exposed passages, short stretches of climbing (I) might be necessary.

Dangers

Almost all of the walks run along clear tracks or well-laid paths which are waymarked frequently with paint or sign-posted. Some high mountain walks and summit ascents lead across challenging terrain with exposed paths and over steep scree or rocks and boulders. The crossing of streams is mostly on footbridges or bridges; particular care should be taken on slippery and loose stones in streams where there is no bridge. As always in the mountains you should also take into account in the Pyrenees the possibility

Mist on the narrow summit of Petit Vignemale.

of sudden changes in the weather with a drop in temperature and the onset of snow, mist or strong winds. This is especially the case on walks in the high mountains and on summits. Remember to take the appropriate equipment which will provide effective protection and to make careful preparations for every walk. If there's a threat of thunderstorms in high summer, you will need to set out on the walk early enough to try and avoid them.

Equipment

The usual hiking gear – sturdy footwear and practical clothing – is essential on every walk. It should offer you enough comfort in the heat, at the same time protect you against the rain, cold and wind. Adequate sun protection is very necessary in the summer. Walking poles are especially recommended on steep and scree-covered ground. Be sure to take enough water and food, especially on long walks and in the high mountains, and even if there's a staffed hut on the way.

Maps (the best to a scale of 1:25,000) not only prove useful if you need to check your direction, but they also help in distinguishing the surrounding peaks and valleys.

Maps

The hiking maps of the Institut Géographique National (IGN) can be recommended unreservedly. At a scale of 1:25 000, they give you a great amount of detail. Similarly, carte de randonnées at a scale of 1:50 000, offer a reliable basic start.

The following maps (IGN; 1:25 000) cover the walks:

– LOURDES (1647 ET): Walk 1
– VIGNEMALE (1647 OT): Walks 2-10, 18
– GAVARNIE (1748 OT): Walks 10-17, 19-26
– NÉOUVIELLE (1748 ET): Walks 27-34
– BAGNÈRES-DE-LUCHON (1848 OT): Walks 35-44
– AULUS-LES-BAINS (2048 OT): Walks 45-50

Walking times

The time details contain the real walking time at a moderate pace and do not include breaks and other stops. The actual length of time that the walk takes depends, of course, on one's individual walking speed and fitness and there not being any unforeseen complications.

Refuges (huts)

The concentration of huts in the hiking area is very good. Many of the staffed refuges are run by the CAM (Club Alpin Français). They are, as a rule, open in the summer months from June to September and sometimes in May and October at weekends. Outside the summer season most of the refuges still have a limited number of overnight places available, but they are not staffed at these times.

Refuge de Baysselance (→ Walk 18).

Overnight bookings should always be made in advance by telephone. For each of the huts described along the way, details are given about their opening times, number of beds (B) and telephone numbers. These details can easily change since the exact opening times usually depend on up-to-date snow conditions. Information can be obtained at any time from the tourist information offices.

Access

Hiring your own car is the best option for most of the walks. There are only bus connections in the larger towns in the central valleys and then only with a very restricted timetable. The smaller mountain valleys have been developed with good roads so that most of the starting points can be reached easily.

In the summer season from 1. July to 15. September access and parking at the various starting points are either restricted or even controlled. At present this is true of:

– GAVARNIE: at the entrance to the town.
– CIRQUE DE TROUMOUSE: toll road to the car park of the Cirque.
– CAUTERETS: pay car park.
– NÉOUVIELLE: obligatory pay car park (9.30 – 18.30) at Lac d'Orédon. From here there's a shuttle bus every 30 minutes to Lac d'Aubert.

Protection of nature

Please take note on every walk of the general code of good conduct intended for the protection of the mountains. Special rules are in existence in

Precious plants under the protection of nature.

the Parc National des Pyrénées and the nature reserves of Néouville and Mont Valier. Information boards along the hiking paths and at the park boundaries give you the details of the individual regulations. The tourist offices also have information brochures available.

Long distance paths

There are two hiking paths available for walking through the Central Pyrenees: the Grande Randonnée No. 10 (GR10) and the Haute Randonnée Pyrenéenne (HRP). The GR10 is a very well laid and maintained path touching on areas and villages in the most beautiful landscapes. With an ideal combination of valley and hill paths it runs along the edge of the border mountains as well as through big valleys so that you have to walk over numerous passes. It is aimed at skilled mountain hikers and in summer doesn't usually require any special equipment like crampons and ice axes. Many sections of the path only run at a moderate altitude and are therefore often possible from early to late in the season.

The HRP runs close to the central massif and even crosses the border ridge. It goes through the French national park and then changes over into the Spanish mountains where it continues as far as the Val d'Aran. As a high mountain path which also ventures at times into the 3000 metre zone and sometimes goes over rough and steep terrain, it is reserved for skilled mountain walkers. Even during the summer you have to be prepared for snowfields in exposed locations on the HRP, which demand the appropriate equipment.

Tips for long distance walkers

Thanks to the excellent network of paths, there's almost no limit to the combination of several day hiking tours over mountain passes and through valleys. Because of the propensity of huts, multi-day walks can easily be divided up into manageable stages and very varied round walks are also possible. Several walks in this guide go onto the top of passes from where there are good, pleasant adjoining paths into neighbouring valleys. Those particularly worth mentioning are Walks nos. 7, 9, 10, 15, 16, 17, 18, 21, 25, 27, 36, 46, 48.

Amongst the classic walks over the Spanish side of the mountains, two are worth a special mention – the walk over the Brèche de Roland (Walk 14) to the Refugio de Goriz at the foot of Monte Perdido and the crossing of the Port de Benasque (Walk 42) to the Refugio de la Renclusa on the Maladeta massif.

The absolute classic: the walk over the Brèche de Roland.

Hiking in the French Central Pyrenees

Geography
The French Central Pyrenees takes up a magnificent position in the more than 400km long mountain range between the Mediterranean and the Atlantic. The highest peaks are concentrated here but the only ones named are Balaïtous (3146m), Vignemale (3298m), Pic Long (3192m) and Pic de Maupas (3109m), and the huge mountain basins of Gavarnie, Estaubé and Troumouse in the Parc National des Pyrénées. Apart from the Néouvielle nature reserve, the great majority of the French 3000ers are on the main ridge that, at the same time, forms the border with Spain. Numerous passes with an average height of 2500m connect the French to the Spanish valleys. The whole area is abundant with streams, rivers and mountain lakes of which many are used to generate electricity. The wonderful landscape of lakes in the Vallée du Marcadau and in the Néouvielle region is especially worth a mention.

A little bit of geology of the French Central Pyrenees
The oldest rocks of the French Central Pyrenees are over 500 million years old. They form the greatest part of the central axis of the mountain chain and date from a long phase of creation in the course of which a layer of marine

Looking at rock at Lac de Gaube.

sediment was laid down on the floor of a shallow sea. When, 350 million years ago, molten material in the earth's mantle pushed to the top, there were strong tensions in the earth's crust which resulted in the breaking of the sedimentary shell. The submerged marine layers for the most part melted together with the magma and formed the granite of Cauterets and Néouvielle. More resistant or remote layers, on the other hand, melted only in part and formed very different metamorphic rocks, as are to be found in the Cirque de Troumouse today.

During the so-called Variscan formation of the mountains, which began 300 million years ago, the original material of the Pyrenees was raised to a mountain plinth stretching out in a long line which is referred to as the axis of the Pyrenees. As a result of a reversal of the lifting process and the creation of a large rift valley, the sea flooded the mainland. In the course of time the newly created layers of sediment were transformed into limestone which was laid down like a huge cover over the original rock. The present alpine formation of the Pyrenees began 35 million years ago. Through the enormous pressure of the Iberian islands against the continental plate, the original mountain base was folded upward again and the youngest deposits of limestone (up to 1000m in thickness) came with it to the surface and this is especially evident at specific locations on the north face of the Taillón. The distortions of the rock connected to the alpine folding didn't only have an effect on the granite which was again broken up and pushed aside, but also affected the loosening of the younger limestone surface of the mountain base. This was displaced, like the surface of the Gavarnie and Monte Perdido, to the south and thrown upwards many times so that extreme distortions were formed in the rock layers. These are especially conspicuous in the Cirque de Gavarnie.

With the youngest glacial phase began the shaping of the actual mountains. There are plenty of opportunities for studying the landscape-sculpting activity of the glaciers in the form of mountain basins, stepped valleys, moraines, hollows on the slopes with lakes and striated granite boulders on the walks. Only some very small remaining glaciers can be found in the central area, the most important of which in the Vignemale and Marboré massifs.

Vegetation

For hundreds of years the French Central Pyrenees was a favourite area for scientific study and research by botanists. The immense diversity of flora also prompted many mountain pioneers to make a comprehensive study of the indigenous plant world. Louis Ramond, the first ascentionist of Monte Perdido in 1802, always used his expedition for the general purpose of botanical studies. The discovery and description of the endemic Pyrenean violet – Ramondia pyrenaica – dates back to him. The various climates, the alignment of the mountain ridges and valleys as well as the geological sub-

Foxglove.

stance, are responsible for a rich variety of species and 150 endemic plants have been identified in the wider area of the national park. In certain of the granite areas like Néouvielle, the alpine rose is a predominant and often luxuriant plant. Depending on the areas of vegetation there are Pyrenean lilies, yellow gentian, Pyrenean valerian, Turk's cap lily and foxglove at altitudes between 800 to 1700m, in the sub alpine region of 1700 to 2300 you will find iris, long-leaved saxifrage and violets, and in the alpine areas above 2300m, gentians, campanula and petrocallis pyrenaica.

Many of the valleys and hillsides are densely wooded. Norway spruce, uncinate pine and silver fir are the dominant representatives amongst the conifers while some delightful deciduous forests consist mainly of beech trees.

Fauna

The rich diversity in species in the animal world is widespread and it ranges from vultures to lynx.

It is most unlikely that you will ever see a lynx close to, but the chances of seeing a bird of prey are much higher. Amongst the birds of prey nesting in the Central Pyrenees are the griffon vulture, the black vulture and the impressive bearded vulture which has a wingspan of up to three metres. Only a few of these bearded vultures nest within the national park in contrast to the Spanish side. There's also a small population of golden eagles.

Lovers of butterflies get their money's worth.

Frequently found, on the other hand, are the unmistakable marmots that were re-introduced successfully as recently as 1948 after a long period of virtual extinction. Chamoix have been badly decimated by hunting, but in the protected zones of the national park they have reappeared in relatively large numbers.

Now and then you will also come across snakes on your walks and together with the harmless vipers there might also be a few poisonous adders or asp vipers amongst them.

With more than 125 species, the Central Pyrenees is a real paradise of birds. Particularly common are the alpine jackdaws and the red-beaked crow that have a rough call and perform unusual aerobatics.

National parks and nature reserves

The Parc National des Pyrénées, established in 1967, forms a relatively narrow strip along the border

The Pyrenean salamander loves clear springs.

with Spain. With a surface area of 457 sq. km. it encompasses six large valleys and the largest massifs and peaks of the French Pyrenees. In its present designated area the national park covers a large part of the Central Pyrenees. As its main task it is concerned with the protection and preservation of the rich diversity of natural mountain landscape and takes into consideration the recreational requirements of the visitor, hiker and mountain climber. Since 1988 there has been some collaboration with the bordering Spanish Parque Nacional de Ordesa y Monte Perdido.

The adjoining Réserve Naturelle du Néouvielle and the Réserve du Mont Valier in the Haut-Couserans, which directly adjoin the national park in the east, are also under special protection. Both nature reserves were established quite early on, but their surface area is relatively modest in relation to the national park.

Parc National des Pyrénées

59 route de Pau, F-65000 Tarbes

℅ 05.62.44.36.60

E-Mail: pyrenees.parc.national@espaces-naturels.fr

Internet: www.parc-pyrenees.com

In several towns there is a national park information office (Maison du Parc National): Arrens, Cauterets, Gavarnie, Saint-Lary.

Canyoning

Fans of this mountain water sport will also be able to practise their sport in the French Central Pyrenees. However the opportunities are limited due to its high mountain character and the force of the water in the gorges and/or reserved for the experts.

In the larger valley resorts you will find numerous tour organizers who offer mostly guided day trips onto the Spanish side.

Caving

The possibilities for exploring caves are restricted to the limestone regions of the mountains; most mountain schools also offer pot-holing.

Several caves have been made accessible in the interior of the region. The Grottes de Bétharram at St.-Pé-de-Bigorre are the most famous and are open to the public.

Climbing

A number of bolted routes at all grades have been set up in the central valleys. The resident climbing schools offer courses and provide information about the location of the crags and the technical grades.

In Luz-St.-Saveur there's a rock face with 80 routes (information from Maison de la Montagne).

Cycling and mountain biking (VTT)

The foothills and their passes are a paradise for racing cyclists. The sport is extremely popular in France and it is almost impossible to drive over a pass without meeting a group of cyclists. The range of levels is vast, from Tour-de-France passes more gentle pass crossings where you can almost always enjoy marvellous views into the mountains.

Particularly well-known for its scenic beauty and sporting challenges is the Col d'Aspin, together with Col du Tourmalet, Col de Peyresourde, Col de Mente and Col de la Core which have an international reputation. The mostly well-laid forest paths in the foothills give the opportunity for mountain bike trips with wonderful views. Route plans for mountain biking are usually available from most tourist offices.

Paragliding

The mountain ranges located on the central ridge are ideal starting points for paragliders. The sport is practised especially in the larger valleys; popular locations where you will also find flying schools or organizations are Arrens, Luz-St.-Sauveur, Barèges, Luchon.

Skiing and snow-shoeing

In the central area there can be found several skiing centres with lifts and prepared slopes, some of which are Gavarnie, La Mongie, Piau-Engaly, St.-Lary and Luchon. Loipen is also set up for cross-country skiing.

Ski tour fans will find all sorts of opportunities in fantastic surroundings. The same applies to the increasingly popular sport of snowshoeing, which is also possible on many of the routes in this guide.

Wild water rafting

Kajak and rafting are popular water sports that are available in many places and are on offer from numerous organizations. Basically all the rivers of the central and side valleys are navigated.

En route in late winter: ascent to the Brèche de Roland from the Spanish side.

Information and addresses

Information
General tourist information:
Office de Tourisme, 3 cours Gambetta, F-65000 Tarbes ℂ 05.62.51.30.31;
E-Mail: ot.tarbes@wanadoo.fr; www.ville-tarbes.fr

Local tourist offices are located in many of the towns, for example in:
ARRENS: ℂ 05.62.97.49.49; E-Mail: val.dazun@wanadoo.fr
CAUTERETS: ℂ 05.62.92.50.27; E-Mail: espaces.cauterets@caute-rets.com; www.cauterets.com
GAVARNIE/GÈDRE: ℂ 05.62.92.49.10 und 05.62.92.48.05; E-Mail: ot.ge-dre@gavarnie.com; www.gavarnie.com
LUZ SAINT-SAUVEUR: ℂ 05.62.92.30.30; E-Mail: ot@luz.org; www.luz.org
SAINT-LARY-SOULAN: ℂ 05.62.39.50.81; E-Mail: st-lary@wanadoo.fr; www.saintlary.com
BAGNERES-DE-LUCHON: ℂ 05.61.79.21.21; E-Mail: luchon@lu-chon.com; www.luchon.com
SEIX: ℂ 05.61.96.52.90; E-Mail: tourisme@haut-couserans.com; www.haut-couserans.com

Try www.rother.de (WebLinks/GeoLinks) for many useful links.

Mountain rescue
Secours en montagne ℂ 05.62.92.41.41 or Gendarmerie ℂ 17 / fire bri-gade ℂ 18

Campsites and wild camping
There are numerous campsites of varying standards. Local communities also offer sites (camping municipal). Camping at farms is less usual (camp-ing à la ferme). Campsites are usually open from June to September and a few are open all year round.
It is forbidden to camp in the Parc National des Pyrénée and the nature re-serves. You are allowed to put up a tent overnight or if there's a sudden change in the weather if you are at least one hour's walk away from the park boundary.

National holidays and festivals
The main holiday period in the summer begins on 14. July (national holiday) and continues until the end of August. From June to September there are festivals that last several days as well as street theatre, concerts, dance fes-tivals, folk festivals, sporting competitions and guided nature tours. Espe-cially famous is the festival of Gavarnie with theatre productions in the open

air with the Cirque de Gavarnie forming a spectacular backdrop.
The tourist offices distribute a calendar every year with all the events listed.

Opening times
The shops are open weekdays generally from 9.00 to 12.00 and 16.00 to 19.00, Mondays often only in the morning. Bakers are open from 7.30. The exceptions are the large supermarkets that in some places are open all day in the summer season and also Sunday mornings.

Time to travel
The best climatic conditions for hiking are in May and June as well as August and September. The early summer months with their mild temperatures are ideal for hiking although at high altitudes there can still be snowfields. July is characterized by its unstable weather conditions when the Biskaya depressions impinge on the central massif and days of fine weather alternate with periods of cloud cover in the mountains. Typical thunderstorms can build up during the day in summer, which then dissipate in the second half of the day, accompanied by intensive precipitation sometimes in the form of hail. The first falls of snow in the high mountains are possible from October onwards.

The early summer is the best season for hiking.

Telephone
The country code for France is 0033. If you telephone from outside the country you do not need to dial the 0 of the local code.

Hiking and mountaineering clubs
CAF (Club Alpin Français); 24, avenue de Laumière – 75019 Paris
℡ 01.53.72.87.00

Weather forecasts
The weather forecast for several days is on display in the tourist offices. A telephone forecast is available from the Météo-France montagne
℡ 08.92.68.04.04.

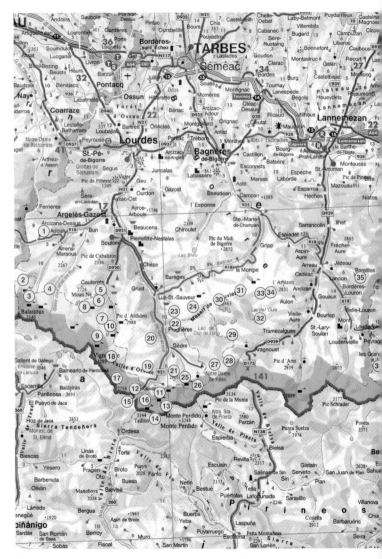

1 Pic de Bazès, 1804m

Curious 'peak' with brilliant views

Col de Couraduque – Col de Bazès – Pic de Bazès and back

Location: Aucun, 847m.
Starting point: car park on the Col de Couraduque, 1367m. Approach from Aucun at the south-western exit of the village along the sign-posted road to the col.
Walking times: car park – Col de Bazès ¾ hr.; to Pic de Bazès ¾ hr.; return

1¼ hrs.; total time 2¾ hrs.
Difference in height: 437m.
Grade: comfortable path as far as the Col de Bazès; steep and at times tough ascent to Pic de Bazès where there are cairns.
Stops and accommodation: Col de Couraduque; Aucun.

The outstanding Belvedère, west of the Vallées d'Arrens, is quickly and easily accessible. On clear days the view is far-reaching and you can see Balaïtous-Massiv in the centre.

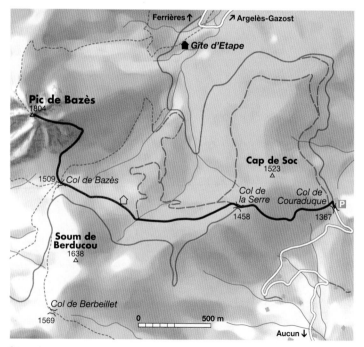

Col and Pic de Bazés.

From the **Col de Couraduque** follow the track descending to the right, next to the restaurant, in a westerly direction. Col de Bazès is indicated on a small yellow walking sign. The track climbs steadily as far as the Col de la Serre, where it splits into two. Don't take the left fork, but go straight on and it levels out and ends at an orange-coloured metal bivouac. The softly curved col lies beyond and the strikingly formed Pic de Bazès with its sheer flanks up to the col and the broad wooded ridge.

The continuing path is made up of deeply furrowed paths, which all lead to the **Col de Bazès**, 1509m. Once there, it is necessary to follow the inconspicuous path to the north-east which leads up to, and clearly crosses, a scree-strewn slope. With the aid of the cairns you can soon make your way up the rapid ascent to the precipitous ridge of Pic de Bazès. At a height of just under 1600m the path bends noticeably to the left and now ascends a steeper incline in a westerly direction. The steep path up the slope leads you finally past a pre-summit on the right-hand side and through larger boulders onto **Pic de Bazès**, 1804m, which offers a clear and far-reaching view of the Val d'Azun mountain range.

2 Lac de Pouey-Laün, 2346m

Meadows of flowers and a lake surrounded by mountains

Lac du Tech – Pla d'Artigou – Lac de Pouey-Laün and back

Location: Arrens, 877m.
Starting point: car park at Lac du Tech, about 100m before the campsite at the southern end of the lake, 1207m. Access from Arrens on the D105 (sign-posted Lac du Tech).
Walking times: Lac du Tech – Pla d'Artigue 1¼ hrs.; Pla d'Artigue – Lac de

Pouey-Laün 2¾ hrs.; return 3 hrs.; total time 7 hrs.
Difference in height: 1139m.
Grade: long walk with big height variations on a good hiking path (clearly positioned cairns); steep ascents.
Refreshments: campsite at the lake; Arrens.

Lac Pouey-Lahun, Pouey-Laün, Pouey-La-Hun or perhaps even Poey-La-Hont as the French Pyrenees pioneer Ledormeur preferred? The different ways of writing the name of this solitary lake at the foot of the Estibère peak are as numerous as the views, which you will enjoy during the long but always exciting ascent.

The sign-posted walk starts from the car park at **Lac du Tech** on the right-hand side of the road. An old forest path climbs up between the walnut and pine trees to a fork, where you continue left up along the roadway as per the signpost. This gradually narrows to a footpath that runs along the Rᵃᵘ de la Lie through the forest and smaller clearings. The path keeps close to the stream after a water regulating plant on the left. The wood recedes to make room for the widening of the valley at **Pla d'Artigou** at 1614m. The flat meadow hillsides resemble a botanical garden with its variety of flowers. From June to August yellow gentians, blue monkshood, aquilega, cranesbill, red foxglove, and meadow roses blossom here and much more, complimented by whitebeam, willow, cherry and mountain ash at the edge of the path. After this medley of flowers the valley narrows again and the hillsides become steeper. The path avoids the scree in the valley bottom to the right and quickly winds uphill and crosses to the other side of the stream, which is hidden under lumps of granite. Having passed the R^{nes} de la Lie, the ruins of a dilapidated shepherds' hut on the left, the path immediately comes up to the national park boundary and crosses the stream once more. You are presented with an impressive arena of jagged ridges and peaks with the striking Pic Arrouy in the middle.

The path continues in a westerly direction and climbs up the mountainside on the right of the stream. In a long series of well-positioned bends it runs up the slope to the R^{nes} de Bassia det Pi (trig point) and continues at a gentle gradient across the grassy slopes to the sign-posted national park boundary. The views become clearer during this comfortable ascent, especially out towards the long Crête des Pic du Midi d'Arrens in the east. Again the path begins to climb, running in places over rocks, before turning right and swinging round into the scree valley at the foot of Pic Arrouy. From here it first goes down the right-hand side of the valley, then crosses the stream briefly in order to avoid larger boulders, immediately changes back over onto the right-hand bank and stays there above the little valley of boulders. Soon the peaceful **Lac de Pouey-Laün**, 2346m, appears at the foot of Crête de Monges and Pic Estibère. The granite hilltop on the other side of the stream at the start of the lake, which you can get to without any difficulty, provides a great vantage point for viewing the magnificent scenery.

Lac de Pouey-Laün.

3 Lac de Suyen, 1536m, and Refuge de Larribet, 2060m

Through a charming Pyrenean landscape to the Balaïtous massif with its glaciers

Maison du Parc – Lac de Suyen – Cabane Doumblas – Refuge de Larribet and back

Location: Arrens, 877m.
Starting point: car park at the end of the D105 at the old Maison du Parc, 1470m. Access from Arrens on the D105 past Lac du Tech to the end of the road.
Walking times: Maison du Parc – Lac de Suyen ¾ hr.; Lac de Suyen – Cabane Doumblas ¼ hr.; Cabane Doumblas – Refuge de Larribet 1½ hrs.; return 2 hrs.; total time 4½ hrs.
Difference in height: 590m.
Grade: walk on well-laid paths; cairns to the Refuge de Larribet.
Refreshments: camping at Lac du Tech; Refuge de Larribet.
Refuge: Refuge de Larribet (1.04.-31.09) ;

B: 61 ✆ 05.62.97.25.39.
Alternative: Lacs de Batcrabère, 2182m. From the refuge, head towards the Brèche de Garenère and ascend the crack in the rock (it might be dangerous in the Brèche if there's snow!). After the narrow section you find yourself standing above the small Lac de Batcrabère and the path continues south-westwards through granite boulders and reaches the large Lac de Batcrabère with a view of Pic d'Artouste, Pic Palas, the north side of the Balaïtou and the Crête de la Garenère, which divides the enormous Balaïtous basin. There and back from the Refuge de Larribet, 1½ hrs.

On the way to the Refuge de Larribet.

The valley plain of Lac de Suyen is the destination of the first part of this walk. The charming meadow plateau joins two valleys, which are separated by a ridged foothill of the Balaïtous massif. You discover the wonderful valley of the R^{au} de Larribet and climb up to the refuge of the same name, which, in its attractive location at the foot of the basin shaped granite valley of Balaïtous formed by glaciers, is a favourite walking destination and the starting point for high altitude alpine walks.

The walk begins at the **Maison du Parc** along the sign-posted path. It crosses straight over the valley stream via the bridge and then winds comfortably upwards through fir trees with striking lichen vegetation. Having levelled out, it passes the national park boundary (information board) and quickly approaches the **Lac de Suyen** at 1536m. Keeping close to the bank it goes towards the southern end of the lake and comes to a sign-posted fork. Up left across the valley hillside, a long mule path continues to Port de la Peyre St.-Martin, from which you can cross over into the Spanish Circo de Piedrafita. The path to the refuge stays close to the stream, goes past the plunging Cascade de Doumblas opposite and shortly afterwards reaches the **Cabane de Doumblas**, 1563m. When you reach the shepherds' hut you will see a perfectly built shelter protected by a large rock, called a 'toue', on the other side of the stream.

The path then crosses the Gave d'Arrens over the small bridge. At the immediately following fork, it carries straight on (the left fork goes over to the path which previously turned off to the pass) and begins to wind up the hillside past numerous cairns. As you get nearer to the R^{au} de Larribet the path opens up into charming countryside populated with rhododendrons, birches, mountain ash and pines and culminates in the picturesque area of Le Cloua at 1771m, where a tiny lake lies in a green mountain trough. La Cloua doesn't just denote the granite striations caused by the Balaitous glacier, it also has great importance for the shepherds as a 'barrière', being the narrowest point for bringing cattle down off the mountain.

After this narrow point the valley widens out into a broad plateau of mead-

Clever symbiosis of nature and architecture.

At your destination: Refuge de Larribet.

ows with a meandering stream and scattered granite boulders created by the thrust of the glacier.

To the right of the stream the path now goes through the beautiful high-lying valley, crosses the stream twice on *passerelles* (foot bridges) and passes another rock shelter, Toue de Larribet, on the right. After the level walk through the valley, the last section of ascent zigzags up the hillside and then heads towards the entrance to the valley, interrupted by a firebreak. The path threads its way through the opening and climbs up round steady, quick bends to flatter areas of the slope. With the hut visible above you to the right, the path climbs up further right, goes over the stream on a small wooden bridge, then continues more or less directly up to the **Refuge de Larribet**, 2060m, across undulating hillsides. The summit of Balaitous is actually hidden behind the rocky façade, but the magnificent mountain basin and the jagged crests of the ridge provide plenty of wonderful views.

4 Lac du Plaa de Prat, 1656m

Stroll up to the delightful high meadows and an enchanting lake

Lac d'Estaing – Pont de Plasi – Lac du Plaa de Prat and back

Location: Arrens, 877m.
Starting point: Lac d'Estaing, car park at the south-western end of the lake, 1163m. Approach from Arrens over the Col des Bordères, then along the D103.
Walking times: Lac d'Estaing – Pont de Plasi 1 hr.; Pont de Plasi – Lac du Plaa de Prat 1½ hrs.; return 2¼ hrs.; total time 4¾ hrs.
Difference in height: 493m.
Grade: easy walk with short ascents on good paths.

Refreshments: bar at Lac d'Estaing; Arrens.
Alternative: Lacs de Liantran, 1824m. Just a few steps after the C^ne du Plaa de Prat you come to a fork in the path where you descend left to Pic de Arrouy; stay on the clear path going south, cross 2 branches of a stream on *passerelles* and ascend gently across the grassy slope. After a few bends the path curves to the left and reaches the lakes. Total time there and back from the C^ne du Plaa de Prat, 1 hr.

Lac d'Estaing, much visited in summer, is the start of this easy walk, going through inviting valley meadows, beautiful forests and green pastures and leading up to a higher plateau with its secluded Lac du Plaa de Prat.
At **Lac d'Estaing** cross over the Gave de Labat on the Pont du Pescadou and walk along the old roadway up the valley, with wooded peaks to the left and steep slopes and jagged ridges to the right. Numerous off-shoots branch off from the stream in the broad and marshy valley bottom.

Lac du Plaa de Prat.

The track becomes a distinctive, gentle uphill path and takes you to **Pont de Plasi**, 1323m. Many day-trippers turn back at the exit to the gorge-like narrowing of the valley, to avoid the following steep climb. This starts on the other side of the bridge with some short bends, but soon becomes less steep and continues through wonderful beech and fir forests.

After a straight section the path soon begins to zigzag again and the forest thins out. The path descends a little to go round a rocky slope and for the time being stays at the same level above the stream, which is automatically controlled by a regulator tank.

As the valley widens you head towards a gentle sloping terrace, which takes you over to La Cétira valley plain after the national park boundary. Go past the 'Toue de la Cétira', the shepherds' hut installed under a boulder on the left, and then Lac de Langle, which is only adequately filled when the snow melts. From here the gradient increases again and the path winds up to the next plain and arrives at **Lac du Plaa de Prat**, 1656m. On the left bank of the lake, it continues further to the *cabane* which lies on the edge of the pretty valley meadow, threaded with streams.

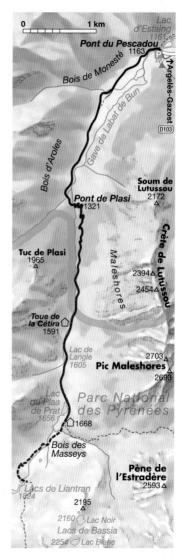

5 'Chemin des cascades' in the Val de Jéret

Impressive waterfalls one after the other

La Raillière – Pont d'Espagne and back

Location: Cauterets, 913m.
Starting point: car park at Pont de la Raillère, 1048m. Approach from Cauterets on the D920 in the direction of Pont d'Espagne.
Walking times: Pont de la Raillère – Pont d'Espagne 1½ hrs.; return 1¼ hrs.; total time 2¾ hrs.
Difference in height: 448m.
Grade: GR10 walk on a broad track; some steep ascents, wet rock in places.
Refreshments: Pont d'Espagne; La Raillière.
Tip: if you want to make the walk an easy

one, use the bus-shuttle between Cauterets – La Raillière – Pont d'Espagne. Timetable (summer 2002): from Cauterets 8.00, 10.00, 12.00, 14.00, 16.00, 18.00; from Pont d'Espagne 9.00, 11.00, 12.30, 15.00, 17.00, 19.00. Bus stop near the Télécabine building.
It is advisable to do this walk in the given direction because the rock is occasionally wet on the descent making it more unpleasant.
Information office at the lift station.
Linking tip: see Walk 6: to the Refuge Wallon.

The walk along the Gave du Marcadau is a refreshing approach to the well-known Marcadau valley. Passing through mixed forests you can marvel at huge waterfalls really close at hand and the massive amount of water in the valley is particularly evident here. The walk finishes at the famous Pont d'Espagne, the starting point for walks into the interior of the Marcadau valley.

The sign-posted hiking path starts at the **Pont de la Raillère** opposite the Griffons thermal baths, where the long Mauhourat waterfall puts you in the right mood. The typical smell of sulphur and the red-coloured rock indicates that this is the source of a thermal spring containing sulphurous water. A bit further on you will notice the slope covered in granite boulders on the right, which is a collection of fallen rocks from Pic de Péguère. After the Cascade d'Escane-Gat the path passes close to the Cascade du Ceriset, which thunders down between narrow rocks, and then leads away slightly from the stream, goes round a sheer drop then gets closer

to the Gave again. To the right a path branches off and ascends Pic de Péguère. Further along the stream, past a bridge on your left, you go through a dense wood of huge fir trees and then beech trees. This is followed by the Cascade de Pouey-Bacou, where you climb up to the vertex and shortly afterwards arrive at the comparatively modest Cascade de L'Ours, from where a bridge leads over to the road opposite. Immediately afterwards you come to another bridge and beyond that, the fast falling Cascade de Boussès, which is constantly surrounded by a fine mist. The path zigzags up above the waterfall, then descends slightly and runs along beside the level and strangely tame stream. You can see the Plateau de Pountas and its car park through the trees on the other side. You eventually go through pretty clearings with meadows riddled with streams until you reach the famous **Pont d'Espagne**, 1496m, which spans the dramatic Gave. Those who wish to return by bus should cross over the bridge to the other side and take the track back to the car park.

Views of unspoiled nature on the 'path of the cascades'.

6 Through the Vallée du Marcadau to the Refuge Wallon, 1865m

On an old path over the pass into the heart of the Marcadau region

Pont d'Espagne – Pont d'Estalounqué – Refuge Wallon and back

Location: Cauterets, 913m.
Starting point: car park on the Plateau de Pountas, 1459m. Approach from Cauterets on the D920.
Walking times: Pont d'Espagne – Pont d'Estalounqué 1½ hrs.; Pont d'Estalounqué – Refuge Wallon 1 hr.; return 2¼ hrs.; total time 4¾ hrs.
Difference in height: 406m.
Grade: problem-free walk. Roadway at first, then a pleasant hiking path.
Refreshments: Pont d'Espagne; Refuge Wallon.
Refuge: Refuge Wallon (1. June – 1. October); B: 120, ✆ 05.62.92.64.28 / 05.61.85.93.43
Tip: information office in the building of the lift station.
Alternative: return from Pont du Cayan on the other bank of the river.
At the fork in the path to the 'Circuit des lacs' you change over to the other side of the Gave du Marcadau across the Pont de Cayan, then go immediately right down the valley. Always keep to the valley path that leads back to the Refuge du Clot.
Linking tip: see Walk 5: in the Val de Jéret.

Marcadau means *la place du marché* (market place) where the Spanish and French inhabitants of the border valleys still met to trade as late as the beginning of the 20th Century. The magnificent Gave du Marcadau has today become one of the classic walks in the national park.

At the **car park** go through the lift station building and100m further on (signpost to 'Pont d'Espagne par les passerelles') take the footpath as a short-cut, instead of the road to the Pont d'Espagne. From there, go back on the road up to the Refuge du Clot, where the actual walk through the valley be-

At your destination: the Refuge Wallon.

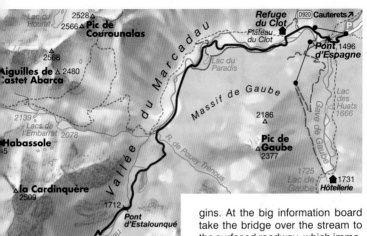

...gins. At the big information board take the bridge over the stream to the surfaced roadway, which immediately splits into two. Take the track to the right going directly along the riverbank and enjoy the pretty spectacle of ledges and rapids. Keeping to this side of the stream, the path pushes on to the asphalt roadway, which straightaway becomes a stony track. Follow the lively Gave du Marcadau through the enormously wide valley bed, passing occasional pines, large blocks of granite and rhododendron bushes on the way.

The path branches off in two directions after a small bridge over a side-stream. The Circuit des Lacs (see Walk 8) begins on the right. The broad valley path climbs up to the left, goes round the steep river bank and makes its way comfortably up and down through pine forests to the **Pont d'Estalounqué**, 1712m. On the other side of the stream walk through pretty meadows, then go uphill round step-like bends and pass the Fontaine des Espagnols. After a small pasture the path rises again where you will notice that gnarled pines and granite rock characterize the scenery. The valley quickly opens up into a wide basin where the various side valleys run together from all possible directions. The sign-posted path to Lac and Col d'Arratille (see Walk 7) turns off left. However you go straight on, briefly climbing again before reaching the **Refuge Wallon**, 1865m, shortly afterwards.

7 Lac d'Arratille, 2247m

To the deep blue glacial lake at the foot of the Grand Pic d'Arratille

Refuge Wallon – Lac d'Arratille and back

Location: Cauterets, 913m.
Starting point: Refuge Wallon, 1865m. Approach and path to the refuge see Walk 6.
Walking times: Refuge Wallon – Lac d'Arratille 2¼ hrs.; return 2 hrs.; total time 4¼ hrs.
Difference in height: 382m.
Grade: well-used hiking path; way-markings on stones.
Refreshments: Refuge Wallon.
Refuge: Refuge Wallon (1.06.-1.10.); B: 120; ✆ 05.62.92.64.28 / 05.61.85.93.43.

Alternative: Col d'Arratille, 2528m. Very beautiful viewpoints of the western Vignemale massif and upper valley of the Rio Ara. Keep right at the lake and go round a large recess of the lake, then past some tiny lakes and southwards (cairns as waymarkers) through the cirque towards the scree slopes that cover the valley slopes. The path now ascends steeply round bends up to Lac du col d'Arratille, keeps flat on the left of the lake and comes to the Col d'Arratille. There and back from Lac d'Arratille, 1½ hrs.

The pretty cirque lake at the foot of Pics d'Arratille is in an area of geographical interest, where granite and sediment rock meet. The granite, which is resistant to glacier erosion, formed a natural dam to the outflow of melt water that collected in a shallow slate and limestone basin.

Walking from the **Refuge Wallon** head down the valley for a while to the sign-posted fork to Lac d'Arratille. Go right there and then over small bridges, one after the other, across the Gave de Marcadau and the Gave d'Arratille. On the left of the stream walk up the hilly valley up a comfortable gradient. The path leads you over broad hillsides that are running with small rivulets. The soft granite hillocks with their striking patterns are evidence of intense glacial activity that also shaped this wide valley. Carry on along the Gave d'Arratille for a while until the path turns off left to avoid the steep rising of the valley. It then winds quickly up the slope to a side-stream where the path rapidly zigzags uphill. Having arrived at the threshold of the valley, cross the stream and there's another sheer section of the hillside ahead of you that you now embark upon in a south-easterly direction. Crossing granite terrain repeatedly with the aid of cairns, the path heads towards the valley stream which cascades down from the upper valley in a pretty waterfall. It then curves uphill and continues across gentle slopes to the wooden bridge over the stream, which has carved a groove into the rocky bed. A few steps further and you reach **Lac d'Arratille**, 2247m.

Waterfalls along the path.

8   The Circuit des lacs in the Vallée du Marcadau

Fascinating round walk through the lake and mountain scenery of the inner Marcadau valley

Pont d'Espagne – Refuge Wallon – Lac du Pourtet – Pont de Cayan – Pont d'Espagne

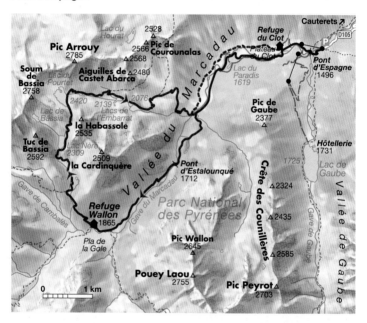

Location: Cauterets, 913m.

Starting point: car park on the Plateau de Pountas, 1459m. Approach from Cauterets on the D920 as far as the car park.

Walking times: Pont d'Espagne – Refuge Wallon 2½ hrs.; Refuge Wallon – Lac du Pourtet 2 hrs.; Lac du Pourtet – Pont de Cayan 2 hrs.; Pont de Cayan – Pont d'Espagne ¾ hrs.; total time 7¼ hrs.

Difference in height: 961m.

Grade: very long round walk with big height variations. Comfortable hiking path as far as the Refuge de Wallon; then along a mainly distinct path with sections of steep ascent; at times over boulders. Cairns.

Refreshments: Pont d'Espagne; Refuge Wallon.

Refuge: Refuge Wallon (1.06.-1.10.); B: 120, ✆ 05.62.92.64.28 / 05.61.85.93.43.

Marvellous view of the mountain range and side valleys of the Marcadau valley.

You can link the valley walk to the Refuge Wallon with a mountain walk that offers great views, connecting Lac Nère, Lac due Poutet and Lacs de l'Embarrat. The lakes, surrounded by a prominently rocky landscape, nestle like glimmering pearls in mountain hollows at various levels. With its far-reaching views over the Marcadau valley, the Circuit des lacs belongs to one of the most beautiful and impressive walks in the region.

The valley walk to the **Refuge Wallon**, 1865m, described in Walk 6, forms the first part of this walk. The climb to the lakes starts from the old hut building. A signpost to Lac Nère indicates the first destination. The path immediately starts to climb up through sparse pine forests and continues across valley slopes until it reaches the fork in the direction of Gave de Cambalés valley and the lakes of the same name. Stay on the path that goes straight on, go past a trig point and begin climbing up the slope round long-drawn-out bends.

The higher you get, the more complete the magnificent panorama becomes of the mountain range and side valleys of the Marcadau valley. The path crosses a stream, winds up through granite hillocks and gets nearer to the wild stream from Lac Nère, which it crosses over to the other side of the rocky slope and there begins the ascent to Lac Nère. The view over the Vignemale Massif opens up to the south-west, but you head to the northern side of the lake. From here the path begins to climb again and makes its way up across gentian-covered slopes.

After a bend in the path you are suddenly confronted with the jagged rock wall of the Aiguilles du Pic Arroy, which drops away to the lake. Only the short climb up the sheer slope separates you now from **Lac du Pourtet** at 2420m. The path now leads along the bank through bits of granite (cairns) and straight up the steep bank until it turns right, a few metres from the drainage stream, indicated by cairns. Don't make the mistake of taking the apparently obvious path going straight on and over the stream. Turning slightly, you soon see the wide curving path up the slope on the left side of the valley, which takes you up to the next lakes. The path then goes over the gully of the R^{au} du Pourtet, which drains off from time to time in summer, and then continues steadily down the valley and past two tiny lakes.

Continuing downhill through the increasingly broader and greener valley where the stream begins to flow again, you arrive at a signpost. Straight on takes you to Lac d'Ilièou, but you head down the hill in the direction of Plateau de Cloth until you arrive at the first and quite shallow lake of Lacs de l'Embarrat. The larger lake follows immediately, after which the much more level path turns into the Marcadau valley before ascending the hillside again.

Head downhill again through pretty hilly countryside where granite boulders, rivulets and above all rhododendrons dominate the scenery and with the valley and the jagged mountain ridges opposite. At another fork in the path carry on downhill to the right and follow a series of quick bends that bring you rapidly down to the valley bottom. Passing through forests of pine and fir trees, the path joins the roadway at **Pont du Cayan** that runs along the Gave du Marcadau to the left and leads back to **Pont d'Espagne** and the car park. Alternatively, you can return along the path to the right of the river.

Lac de l'Embarrat.

9 Lac de Gaube, 1731m, and Refuge des Oulettes de Gaube, 2151m

A popular lake and the glacier sloped north face of the Vignemale massif

Plateau de Pountas – Lac de Gaube – Refuge des Oulettes de Gaube and back

Location: Cauterets, 913m.
Starting point: car park on the Plateau de Pountas, 1459m. Approach from Cauterets on the D920 as far as the car park.
Walking times: Plateau de Pountas – Lac de Gaube 1 hr.; Lac de Gaube – Refuge des Oulettes de Gaube 1¾ hrs.; return 2½ hrs.; total time 5¼ hrs.
Difference in height: 692m.
Grade: GR10 all the way, marked red and white. Effortless walk as far as Lac de Gaube; technically easy, but long walk to the refuge.
NB: the Vignemale massif is a natural focal point for storms. In unstable weather con-

ditions there's the possibility of sudden storms that bring about a drop in temperature.
Refreshments: Hôtellerie at Lac de Gaube; Refuge des Oulettes de Gaube.
Refuge: Refuge des Oulettes de Gaube (15.5.-30.10.); B: 120; ℓ 05.62.92.62.97.
Tip: the Télésiège de Gaube (chair lift) takes you practically the whole way from the valley to the lake. From the mountain station there's a 15minute flat dirt track to the northern end of the lake.
The descent from the mountain station into the valley is bleak and not to be recommended.
Information office in the lift station.

Lac de Gaube.

Lake Gaube at the entrance to the valley is an idyllic contrast to the seemingly unapproachable rock and ice of the Vignemale. The lake is a very popular destination and many enjoy the surrounding mountain countryside from the lakeshore in the summer. The walk through the Gaube valley to the refuge is a fascinating experience. The insurmountable Vignemale valley and its vertical cliffs of over 3000m, its steep gullies and low hanging glaciers seem to be in wide screen perspective, while the glacial streams meander through marshlands on the valley floor.

From the **Plateau de Pountas** car park, head through the lift building and follow the road to the bridge over the Gave de Gaube, sign-posted 'Lac de Gaube'. The GR10 winds steeply up a stepped gradient, through pine forests rich in lichen, and later mixed forests. Occasionally you catch a glimpse of waterfalls through the forest. A low-lying area with numerous types of flowers, marshland and the small Lac des Huats lies beneath the path. Cross two small streams, one after the other coming from the left, and walk between striking blocks of granite and over an open root system at first on the level and then ascending slightly until you reach **Lac de Gaube**, 1731m, with the restaurant on the left.

The GR10 to the Refuge de Gaube crosses the drainage stream and goes across to the other side of the lake, where you reach the track from the Télésiège de Gaube

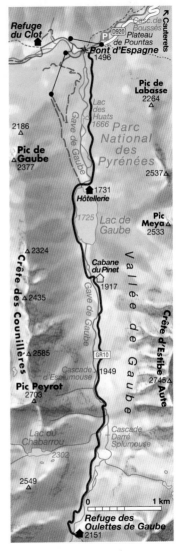

The Gave des Oulettes transports the melt water from the Vignemale glacier.

View from the Refuge of the north face of the Vignemale.

mountain station. You then follow the partly scree-covered bank (beware falling rocks) to the south side of the lake, which extends into a delightful area of meadows, pines and rivulets. Ignore the first bridge over the valley stream on the left and only when the gorge narrows should you cross over to the other side. After a short but steep climb, leave the C^{ne} due Pinet behind, take the gentle cart track which heads towards a valley ledge with the pretty cascades of the Esplumouse waterfall. Climb further up the valley until you find yourself above the waterfall. If you look back you can get a great view of Lac de Gaube, whilst the long descending Vignemale glaciers glint in the foreground. Take the level path along the stream, then cross over it on a wooden *passerelle* (foot bridge) and walk through charming water meadows and rich green fields. Another ledge where the path goes down through an opening, then over the ledge to reach the plateau again. You end up on a wide, green valley plateau and follow the stream that runs through it with its many branches. Passing a small bridge on the left, the path swings round onto the right side of the valley. Some steep bends take you up the last difficult ledge of the valley and you reach a fork in the path next to a *passerelle*. Walk across left to the **Refuge des Oulettes de Gaube**, 2151m, which sits on a plinth of rock.

10 Refuge and Lac d'Estom, 1804m

Peaceful walk through picturesque Vallée de Lutour

La Fruitière – Lac d'Estom and back

Location: Cauterets, 913m.
Starting point: car park at the Hôtellerie La Fruitière, 1371m. Approach from Cauterets on the D920, turn off left after La Raillière (after the hairpin bends) in the direction of La Fruitière.
Walking times: La Fruitière – Lac d'Estom 2 hrs.; return 1¾ hrs.; total time 3¾ hrs.
Difference in height: 433m.
Grade: easy walk on clear paths; some steep sections of ascent from time to time.
Refreshments: Hôtellerie La Fruitière at the car park; Refuge d'Estom.
Refuge: Refuge d'Estom (1.6.-30.9.); B: 30; ✆ 05.62.92.07.18.

This is a classic walk along the Gave de Lutour and often used in the summer. It goes through a charming valley, dominated by the Labas peaks and l'Ardiden. Chamois and marmots are as common as the colourful rhododendrons.
At Hôtellerie **La Fruitière** take the wide valley path, which immediately leads over the bridge to the other side of the stream. Keeping close to the stream head up the valley on a pleasant gradient, through pretty pastures. The steep and stony valley slopes opposite are a favourite resting place for the chamois, especially in the morning. Accompanied by rhododendron and juniper shrubs, with some solitary pine trees, the path heads towards a valley ledge over which a wide waterfall cascades from the Gave de Lutour.
After a short climb you arrive at the

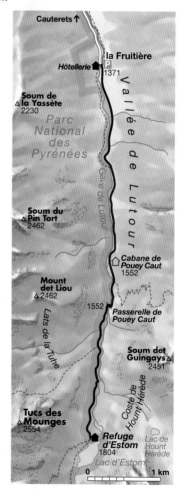

Cⁿᵉ de Pouey Caut: an extraordinary shepherds' hut.

next plain where the picturesque countryside resumes with the meandering stream.

Passing the Cⁿᵉ de Pouey Caut you come to the conspicuous shepherds' hut on the left with its semi-circular roof, which is sheltered by a huge boulder about the size of a house. A bit further on the left a path leads up to the Refuge Russell, however you need to continue along the valley and immediately cross over the stream on the wooden bridge. Continue on the level for a while before the path begins to slowly ascend and then steepen up near the broadly fanned waterfall ahead. Following the engorged and fast flowing stream you wind up through the forest, passing a waterfall that is split into two by a boulder and head away from the stream after another waterfall. After a short climb up an open slope you finally reach the **Refuge d'Estom**, 1804m, at the northern end of the lake.

11 Round walk through the Cirque de Gavarnie

Away from the popular trail to the famous valley head of Gavarnie

Gavarnie – Plateau de Pailla – Hôtellerie du Cirque – Prade St.-Jean – Gavarnie

Location: Gavarnie, 1360m.
Starting point: pay car park at the entrance to Gavarnie.
Walking times: Gavarnie – Plateau de Pailla 1½ hrs.; Plateau de Pailla – Hôtellerie du Cirque 1 hr.; Hôtellerie du Cirque – Prade St.Jean ½ hr.; Prade St.Jean – Gavarnie ½ hr.; total 3½ hrs.
Difference in height: 382m.
Grade: easy round walk on clear paths; steep approach to the Plateau de Pailla, slightly exposed in places from there to the Cirque.

Refreshments: Gavarnie; Chalet ASPTT (Plateau du Pailla); Hôtellerie du Cirque.
Refuge: Chalet ASPTT (1.07.-15.9.); B: 20; ✆ 05.62.92.48.48.
Tip: the walk can also be done in the opposite direction.
Alternative: big cascade in the Cirque de Gavarnie, 1730m. At the Hôtellerie du Cirque follow the roadway into the valley basin. It soon turns into a hiking trail and leads along the left-hand side of the valley to the foot of the 400m high cascade. There and back from the Hôtellerie, ¾ hr.

At the start of Gavarnie (photograph by Lucien Briet, 1895).

Cirque de Gavarnie – the Lourdes of the French Pyrenees! Masses of visitors set off in the summer months and make a pilgrimage into this wonderful valley basin to experience the natural spectacle of the big cascades and the rock faces towering up 1500m. There's no need to describe the overrun quick way along the track beside the valley stream. Instead you can take a very much less used round path that affords you incomparably nicer and more varied perspectives of the unique mountain scenery.

You go through **Gavarnie** to start with and at the height of the campsite and La Bergerie Café cross over onto the other bank of the Gave du Gavarnie on the Pont Brioule and from there go up the valley as far as a house with a signpost to the Refuge des Espuguettes. Turn off left here from the roadway, immediately past a Parc National information sign and ascend the slope along the broad, stony path. Luxuriant meadows of flowers accompany the long, but pleasant zigzag uphill path which brings you to a small hollow in the slope with a fork. Follow the path in the direction of Cirque de Gavarnie through the forest and after the bridge over the valley stream you come to a secluded clearing on the western edge of the **Plateau de Pailla**, 1748m, with a refuge (Chalet ASPTT). The extensive meadow plateau is closed off in the east by the impressive rock faces of the Petit Cirque de Pailla.

The continuing path descends round a few bends, then runs down a gentle incline through a mixed forest and becomes a mountain path with beautiful views high above the valley floor. For a while below greatly overhanging rock, again at the foot of impressive steep walls, continue up the valley mostly on a level or very slightly descending, cross the occasional steep gully and the path runs close to the edge of precipitous slopes. At the end, descend steeply down towards the valley basin. After crossing a side-stream (take care when the water level is high) you arrive at the **Hôtellerie du Cirque**, 1550m.

Hôtellerie du Cirque.

Now turn down the valley and walk along the broad track round three bends. On the fourth bend as well as just after it, two well-trodden paths branch off left and descend through the forest quickly down to the valley stream and meet up again there at the concrete bridge.

Cross over onto the other side of the Gave de Gavarnie and reach the edge of the **Prade St.-Jean**, 1440m. The Gavarnie annual festival games are staged in these idyllic meadows that in summer are covered with crocuses. Walk across the meadows in a northerly direction where the path sometimes becomes indistinct. Cross over several streams on little bridges and head towards a small rocky elevation – the Turon de la Courade – where two big pioneers of the Pyrenees, Schrader and Le Bondidier, are buried. Keep to the left around the rocky hilltop and shortly afterwards take the ascending path left (the descending path joins the valley path) and you quickly meet a cross path. Follow this to the right, through meadows of flowers and with the most beautiful views, as far as the hiking path which goes left to Port de Boucharou (see Walk 16). Continue straight on here to the church of **Gavarnie** where the path ends and the village road starts.

The Grande Cascade plunges down 400m in the mountain basin.

12 Pic de la Pahule, 2292m

On a level with the Cirque de Gavarnie

Col de Tentes – Pic de Tentes – Pic de la Pahule and back

Location: Gavarnie, 1360m.
Starting point: car park at the Col de Tentes, 2208m. Approach from Gavarnie on the D923 in the direction of Port de Boucharo.
Walking times: Col de Tentes – Pic de Tentes ½ hr.; Pic de Tentes – Pic de la Pahule ¾ hr.; return 1 hr.; total time 2¼ hrs.
Difference in height: 115m (with some ascents in between).

Grade: effortless ascent on well-laid paths to Pic de Tentes, afterwards a path along the crest; steep; but short ascent to Pic de la Pahule.
Refreshments: Gavarnie.
Tip: the path to Pic de Tentes has recently been restored after the slope became dangerously eroded. Be sure not to take any shortcuts!

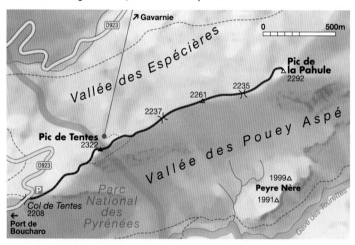

The easiest and quickest way to get a close look at the enormous mountain face of the western Marboré massif is along this ridge path. With the imposing north front of the Taillon with its glaciers opposite, you walk to Pic de la Pahule – a brilliant viewpoint from where you can see the rocky masses and stratum of the Cirque de Gavarnie, shunted into one another, in all their glory.

The path leaves the road opposite the big parking area at the **Col de Tentes**. It zigzags up the mountain ridge in a north-easterly direction, accompanied on the right by the huge north face of the Taillon.

Opposite the Pics de Astazou.

You reach **Pic de Tentes**, 2322m, after only half an hour and then the path descends again and leads gently up and down to the right along the undulating ridge. The nearer you come to the prominent rise of Pic de la Pahule at the end of the crest, the more the Cirque de Gavarnie opens up. On the right below, the beautiful Vallée des Pouey Aspé runs down from Port de Boucharo into the Gavarnie valley.

The path heads towards the left-hand steep flank of the mountain that has great views, climbs it and reaches the flat hilltop and then after a few steps, the 'summit' of **Pic de la Pahule**, 2292m.

The view from Pic des Gabiétous in the east as far as Pics de Astazou to the west of the Marboré chain is breathtaking!

13 Refuge de la Brèche de Roland (Ref. des Sarradets), 2587m

Fantastic high mountain path to a symbol of the Hautes Pyrénées

Col de Tentes – Port de Bouchara – Refuge de la Brèche de Roland and back

Location: Gavarnie, 1360m.
Starting point: car park on the Col de Tentes, 2208m. Approach from Gavarnie on the D923 in the direction of Port de Bouchara.
Walking times: Col de Tentes – Port de Bouchara ½ hr.; Port de Bouchara – Refuge de la Brèche de Roland 2½ hrs.; return 2½ hrs.; total time 5½ hrs.
Difference in height: 379m.
Grade: high mountain walk on HRP path, cairns and red waymarkers. Steep ascent through the arms of the valley at the foot of

the Glacier du Taillon. Be careful of the slippery rocks here – in the afternoon the glacier melt water causes the stream to swell, which makes the crossing awkward. You can expect snowfields at the start of the season; crampons and ice axes are therefore necessary! Information available from the tourist office in Gavarnie.
Refreshments: Gavarnie; Refuge de la Brèche de Roland.
Refuge: Refuge de la Brèche de Roland (1.05.-30.09.); B: 57; ✆ 05.62.92.40.41.

The Refuge de la Brèche de Roland (formerly Refuge des Sarradets named after the peak behind which it is located) was built in 1956 by the French Alpine Club. Built into a 100m high rock wall it lies at the foot of the famous cleft between Taillon and Casque. The sight of the broad cleft is really awe-inspiring and attracts many people who would like a close-up view of this mythical natural monument from the legend of Roland. Even if the location doesn't have especially brilliant views, the walk up to the refuge is a first class experience in itself.

At the **Col de Tentes** walk along the road barred to traffic as far as **Port de Bouchara**, 2270m. The crossing over into the Spanish Valle de Bujaruelo offers a beautiful panorama of the nearby mountain region to the west.

The path to the refuge is waymarked with signposts. It starts off to the east and runs at first without any significant incline at the foot of Pic de Gabiétou, then along the gigantic north face of the Taillon. There are still some spots of glacier remaining on the steep slopes of

the massif. Walk across an extensive high plateau with lots of small islands of flowers standing out between the glacier-strewn rock. On the right the fantastic rocky backdrop of the Taillon and in the foreground the steep Pic des Sarradets accompanies you. The path turns off to the right before a steep valley and ascends steeply. At the following sign-posted fork the left-hand path leads steeply downhill to Gavarnie. Continue uphill and you get nearer to the broad, fast-flowing stream which collects the melt water from the Glacier du Taillon. The path leads to a rock face with a safety chain that secures a section of scrambling on the right of the stream.

(If the stream is flowing fast this section is covered in water and is a bit tricky; in this case cross the stream right at the start on boulders following the red arrows and zigzag up the slope. This alternative joins the path again further up.)

Ascend the steep slope as far as the end of the chain, cross the stream there and move away from it. The path now ascends south-eastwards through boulders, sometimes on loose ground, at the edge of the glacier tongue up to the Col des Sarradets where you will be surprised by a fabulous view of the huge mountains all around you. The Cirque de Gavarnie lies ahead and the series of peaks of the 3000ers – from Pic du Marboré as far as the Casque. It's only a short way along a level path from the small col over to the **Refuge de la Brèche de Roland**, 2587m, where the majestic Brèche de Roland emerges in a particularly impressive manner.

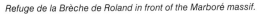

Refuge de la Brèche de Roland in front of the Marboré massif.

14 Brèche de Roland, 2807m, and Taillon, 3144m

Excellent walk to a masterpiece of natural genius and a classic 3000er

Refuge de la Brèche de Roland – Brèche de Roland – Taillon and back

Location: Gavarnie, 1360m.
Starting point: Refuge de la Brèche de Roland, 2587m. For the approach see Walk 13 to the Refuge de la Brèche de Roland.
Walking times: Refuge de la Brèche de Roland – Brèche de Roland ¾ hr.; Brèche de Roland – Taillon 1 hr.; return 1½ hrs.; total time 3¼ hrs.
Difference in height: 557m.
Grade: high mountain walk with a short crossing of a remaining glacier. Depending on the condition of the snow, crampons and ice axes are essential since the whole of the steep slope below the

Brèche can be covered in snow or snow-fields right up into August. Otherwise walking poles might come in handy across the scree-covered terrain.
Only experienced mountain walkers are advised to go the rest of the way to the Taillon if there's snow. The narrow ridge in particular, after the Fausse Brèche, can be very dangerous!
Information from the Office du Tourisme in Gavarnie.
Refreshments: Gavarnie; Refuge de la Brèche de Roland.
Refuge: Refuge de la Brèche de Roland (1.05.-30.09.); B: 57; ✆ 05.62.92.40.41.

Brèche de Roland – *the* destination in the French Pyrenees! Even a famous pioneer of the Pyrenees Henry Russell allowed himself to get carried away with rapturous enthusiasm when he stood on the Brèche de Roland at sunset. If you stand today between the vertical rock faces in the gigantic cleft which is surrounded in legend, you will be equally impressed and fascinated by the majesty of the surrounding rocky landscape (see picture on p.13). The continuing path to the Taillon, the 'easiest' 3000er of the Gavarnie peaks, rounds off a truly wonderful mountain experience with great contrasts in scenery and far-reaching views.

The path is waymarked from the **Refuge de la Brèche de Roland** and cannot be missed. If there's snow on the ground, a few long bends lead up

across the steep slope – if the path is clear of snow you can follow the well-trodden loose path and pass the small remaining glacier near to the foot of the rock walls. Just below the cleft, a few metres of scrambling still awaits you on the rocky elevation and then you are standing in the **Brèche de Roland**, 2807m.

A path sets off on the southern side of the narrow base of the cleft along

View from Taillon.

the western precipices of the Casque to the Refugio de Góriz in the Spanish Valle de Ordesa. In contrast, the path to the Taillon turns to the west and runs along beside the huge south face of Pointe Bazillac. Mostly up a moderate incline and on a good track it passes shelters in the overhanging rock, gets closer to the abrupt end of the rock wall, rises more steeply and heads towards the Doigt de la fausse brèche (finger of the false cleft). Before the rock tower, the path changes over onto the right-hand side of the ridge and then afterwards returns to the southern side where it at first runs just below the ridge for a short way and then along it. The slopes drop steeply away on both sides. Then the ridge becomes wider and goes along the scree-covered ridge of the Taillon, where the path winds uphill. The path soon divides: the direct path, but more strenuous ascent goes more along the left-hand side of the ridge, while the more pleasant path keeps on the right and runs up round bends to the fissured summit ridge on which a clear path leads over left to the highest point of the **Taillon**, 3144m. Splendid views from the summit in all directions!

15 Lakes around the Col des Espécières, 2334m

Revelatory paths across the pass into the Spanish border mountains

Col de Tentes – Col des Espécières – Barranco del Puerto – Port de Boucharo – Col de Tentes

Location: Gavarnie, 1360m.
Starting point: car park am Col de Tentes, 2208m. Approach from Gavarnie on the D923 in the direction of Port de Boucharo.
Walking times: Col de Tentes – Col des Espécières ¾ hr.; Col des Espécières – Barranco del Puerto 1¼ hrs.; Barranco del Puerto – Port de Boucharo 1 hr.; Port de Boucharo – Col de Tentes ½ hr. ; total time 3½ hrs.
Difference in height: 420m.
Grade: effortless round walk on clear paths, some steep sections on the pass.
Refreshments: Gavarnie.

The Col des Espécières and the neighbouring Port de Boucharo formerly played an important role as a cross-over between Gavarnie and Torla in the valley of the Río Ara. From the passes at the foot of Pics de Gabiétous you will enjoy a first-class view of the mountains of the Valle de Bujaruelo with the dramatically formed Sierra de Tendeñera stealing the show. This round walk where you will come across two lakes, one on either side of the border ridge, is an enjoyable trip with changing mountain backdrops.

The described route begins at the **Col de Tentes** at the car park to Lac des Espécières. A grassy path leads you to the round lake where you continue on the right-hand shore towards the slope of the ridge. The path climbs up the steep slope of the col to the **Col des Espécières**, 2334m. The Ibón de Lapazosa lies on the other side and you now descend the slope towards this and continue along the right or left shore of the lake to its outflow. The path at first stays between the stream and the electricity power line, descends across grassy slopes and crosses the stream on the more level hillside and then turns to the south. Cross below the electricity power line and go downhill close to the stream to the valley of the **Barranco del Puerto**, 1990m, where you join the mule track from San Nicolás de Bujaruelo to Port de Boucharo. Follow it to the left, immediately cross the side-stream and with a continuing incline head towards the easily recognizable pass which drops down to the foot of the precipitous Pics de Gabiétous. The path gets a lot steeper before a sheer drop, and then changes over onto the other side of the valley from where it starts to zigzag up to the top of the pass.

Port de Boucharo: view back into Spain.

You reach **Port de Boucharo**, 2270m, from where there's a wonderful view back to Valle de Otal with the limestone peaks of the Sierra Tendeñera you've left behind. When you reach the road on the pass, go left and after a few paces the path turns to the right through the Vallée des Pouey-Aspé down to Gavarnie (see Walk 16). With the huge north face of the Taillon and the increasingly broader summit face of the Cirque de Gavarnie behind you, return to the starting point.

16 Cabane des Soldats, 1954m

A delightful side valley with a marvellous view of the Cirque

Gavarnie – Plateau de Bellevue – Cabane des Soldats and back

Location: Gavarnie, 1360m.
Starting point: pay car park at the entrance to Gavarnie.
Walking times: Gavarnie – Plateau de Bellevue 1 hr.; Plateau de Bellevue – Cabane des Soldats 1 hr.; return 1¾ hrs.; total time 3¾ hrs.
Difference in height: 594m.
Grade: easy walk on an old mule path with some steeper sections.
Refreshments: Gavarnie.
Alternative: Port de Boucharo, 2270m.

From the Cⁿᵉ des Soldats the path continues along the right-hand side of the valley. At first across the level valley bottom, then ascending more steeply round some bends, the path eventually crosses the slope at the head of the valley and finishes at the road which leads from the Col de Tentes. Go along this to the left to the nearby Port de Boucharo where you are afforded a brilliant view of the mountains of the Spanish Valle de Bujaruelo. 1¾ hrs there and back from the Cⁿᵉ des Soldats.

On this walk you meander through the pretty Vallée des Pouey Aspé, which runs down from Port de Boucharo to the valley bottom of the Gave de Gavarnie. The green valley is bordered to the south by mountain formations shaped by glaciers, above which rise the rocky headwalls of Taillon and Pic

Plateau de Bellevue: fabulous viewpoint.

des Sarradets; in the north it is enclosed by the ridge between Pic de Tentes and Pic de la Pahule. Half way along the route you pass the Plateau de Bellevue which certainly does justice to its name. From here there's a wonderful view of the Cirque de Gavarnie.

In **Gavarnie** follow the road which ascends right to the village church and ends there. This is where the old mule path begins which French traders and pilgrims once used to go over into Spain. The broad path runs gently up a steady incline across the valley bottom.

Ignore two narrow paths branching off left and then you come to the start of Les Entortes, a series of bends winding steeply up the slope which, after a flatter section, continues as far as the wide, gentle meadow slopes of the Plateau Bellevue, 1700m. Past the Cne de Pouey Aspé on the right, the path runs across the long-drawn-out plateau in a south-westerly direction until you come to a sign-posted fork where you keep straight on and then head towards the valley made narrow by a projection in the slope. The path runs above the Gave des Tourettes across the slope, then the valley opens up again and gives way to soft meadow slopes with scattered boulders. The Cne des Soldats, with Port de Boucharo above it, are already in sight. It's a leisurely walk along beside the winding stream and past waterfalls which cascade down sheer rock barriers on the south side of the valley. A narrow path turns off left at a fork to the Refuge de la Brèche de Roland while the path you need to take ascends a little and reaches the **Cabane des Soldats**, 1954m. Incidentally, the hut owes its strange name to an old field camp that was set up here during the French revolution to defend the border into Spain from a monarchist incursion.

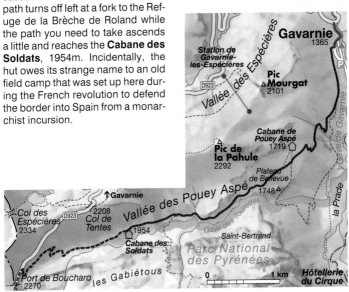

17 Col and Lac de la Bernatoire, 2335m

Through the Vallée de la Canau to the French-Spanish border pass

Barrage d'Ossoue – Cabane de Lourdes – Col and Lac de la Bernatoire and back

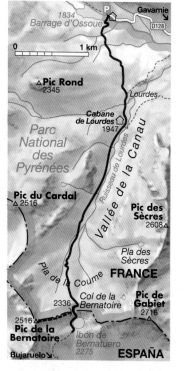

Location: Gavarnie, 1365m.

Starting point: Barrage d'Ossoue, 1834m. From Gavarnie just under 1km on the D923, then continue right along the narrow valley road of the Gave d'Ossoue. It ends before the small reservoir. Parking here. It's a tarmac road at first, but later becomes a track that you can still drive along despite the bumpy sections.

Walking times: Barrage d'Ossoue – Cⁿᵉ de Lourdes 1 hr.; Cⁿᵉ de Lourdes – Col de la Bernatoire 1½ hrs.; Col de la Bernatoire – Lac de la Bernatoire ¼ hr.; return 2¼ hrs.; total time 5 hrs.

Difference of height: 521m.

Grade: almost effortless walk on good paths. Red and white marked GR10 as far as the Cⁿᵉ de Lourdes. Several section with steep ascents.

Refreshments: Gavarnie.

Alternative: Pic de la Bernatoire, 2516m. After the Col de la Bernatoire descend to the right. Problem-free ascent along the border ridge going west to the summit with beautiful views. 1 hr. there and back from the col.

The Vallée de la Canau is one of the neighbouring valleys in the area of Gavarnie, which quickly help you to forget the hustle and bustle around the Cirque de Gavarnie. The hiking path through the peaceful valley leads up to the circular Lac de la Bernatoire, which lies in a deep hollow of the col on the border pass to the Spanish Valle de Bujaruelo.

At the **Barrage d'Ossoue** cross over the stream on the little bridge below the dam and take the sign-posted GR path. After climbing up at first over the grassy hillsides, it levels out and goes in a straight line across the steep slope.

After crossing the slope, steady zigzags bring you up to pastures which you

Lac de la Bernatoire.

head across towards the shepherds' hut. A *passerelle* (foot bridge) leads over a side-stream of the Rᵃᵘ de Lourdes, after which the GR turns off left to Gavarnie. Continue straight on along the path, leave the **Cabane de Lourdes**, 1950m, behind you and now walk along the moderately inclined path beside the stream into the Vallée de la Canau. The gradient increases noticeably and the path climbs swiftly up to the col which falls between the gentle ridge of Pic de la Bernatoire and the sheer rock shoulder of Pic de Gabiet.

The increasingly stony path joins the Pla de la Coume where cairns mark the ascent over the scree-covered slope to the pass. The last section then becomes really steep again before you reach the **Col de la Bernatoire**, 2335m. The dark lake appears as if lying in a volcanic crater in an almost round basin without any visible outlet. The path over the pass goes down to **Lac de la Bernatoire**, 2275m, which you can walk round easily along the path on the right-hand bank.

Be sure to make the short ascent up to the Spanish Puerto de Bernatuara on the opposite side with its view down into the Valle de Bujaruelo!

18 Refuge de Baysselance, 2651m, and Petit Vignemale, 3032m

High walk amongst spectacular scenery into the Vignemale massif

Barrage d'Ossoue – Refuge de Baysselance – Hourquette d'Ossoue – Petit Vignemale and back

The ascent to Pique Longue leads over the Glacier d'Ossoue..

Location: Gavarnie, 1360m.

Starting point: Barrage d'Ossoue, 1834m. Approach from Gavarnie just under 1km on the D923, then continue right along the narrow valley road of the Gave d'Ossoue that ends before the small reservoir. Parking here. It's a tarmac road at first, but later it becomes a track that you can still drive along despite the bumpy sections.

Walking times: Barrage d'Ossoue – Refuge de Baysselance 2½ hrs; Refuge de Baysselance – Hourquette d'Ossoue ½ hr.; Hourquette d'Ossoue – Petit Vignemale ¾ hr.; return 3¼ hrs.; total time 7 hrs.

Difference in height: 1198m.

Grade: moderate walk as far as the Refuge de Baysselance on GR10; several sections of steep ascent. As you continue

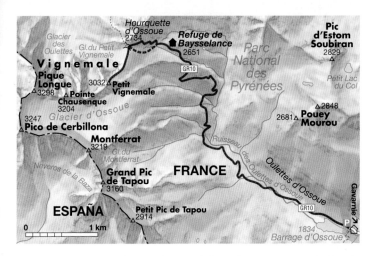

to the Petit Vignemale it becomes a long high mountain walk with considerable variation in height. The ascent to the summit is steep and loose, but without technical problems if there's no snow on the path. The last 'step' to the summit is extremely exposed. In snow or ice the summit ascent is very demanding and crampons and ice axes are absolutely essential. Information from the Office du Tourisme in Gavarnie or at the Refuge de Baysselance.

Warning: during the ascent to the Refuge de Baysselance you come to the Pont de Neige, a snow bridge over a stream which usually lasts all year round. You can expect to find crevasses and sections of severe erosion in summer, which you need to find your way around with care.

Refreshments: Gavarnie; Refuge de Baysselance.

Refuge: Refuge de Baysselance (20.06.-20.09.); B: 70; ☎ 05.62.92.40.25.

Tip: the walk affords you wonderful mountain views even without the climb to the summit of Petit Vignemale.

The Vignemale massif is simply spectacular with its steep rocky flanks and the masses of ice from the various glaciers. You can already see the big Glacier d'Ossoue on this extremely varied walk to the Refuge de Baysselance. The normal route goes across the glacier to the Pique Longue which is, with a height of 3298m, the highest peak in the French Pyrenees. So on the Petit Vignemale you have not only the central massif close-by and the Marcadau valley at your feet, but also a cavalcade of named peaks before your very eyes.

The walk begins at the **Barrage d'Ossoue** on the right of the small reservoir at the signpost for Hourquette d'Ossoue/Refuge Baysselance. It's a leisurely walk along the GR down the valley of the R^{au} des Oulettes d'Ossoue towards the sudden drop into the valley with the big waterfall. Just before that the path changes over onto the other side of the stream on a little concrete bridge and there ascends the valley hillside. At the height of the pretty waterfall some bends take you across the channel of the stream. After that the path descends a short way then immediately ascends again and keeps heading towards a large sheer rock face from which several waterfalls cascade down. At the height of the Barranco d'Ossoue you come to the Pont de Neige, which you can cross over or walk round depending on the condition of the snow bridge. To go round it, descend the bank at some point to the valley stream, cross over the side-stream where it joins the main stream, and climb back up again to the path.

The path now goes up round some steep bends to overcome the deep valley cleft. It then runs at the foot of the small basin formed by the rock wall and continues on the level over to the Barranco d'Ossoue where it goes round a series of bends again. During the hefty climb you can see the reddish rock wall rising in the background of the Crête du Petit Vignemale which continues left in the gray-coloured summit section of the Petit Vignemale. The path swings to the west while in front of you the Glacier d'Ossoue, the biggest glacier of the Vignemale massifs, presents itself. Past two shelters in the rock, the Grottes Bellevue, walk towards a broad scree slope, climb up along its edge and turn off to the north-east again. The hut soon becomes visible on a small elevation as you continue to zigzag uphill. After another bend in the path you follow the stream for a little way, then cross over it and climb up to the **Refuge de Baysselance**, 2651m.

There's a good view of the broad col of the Hourquette d'Ossoue from the hut. You now have two possibilities. Either stay on the faintly marked GR10 which runs gently downhill at first, then quickly gains height on the right-hand slope up several twisty bends and runs horizontally along to the col or keep in the valley along a stony path (cairns) past a pool, then round bends up to the col. At **Hourquette d'Ossoue**, 2734m, continue in a southerly direction and ascend up along the ridge which drops away steeply to the right. The well-trodden bends in the path merge into the widening ridge where there are also paths running parallel uphill. The twisting scree path keeps going up the continuously steady, in places steep incline along the broad ridge of the Petit Vignemale. It finally tapers off at the top with sheer drops on either side and after a few steps over exposed rock you are standing on the narrow summit of the **Petit Vignemale**, 3032m.

Hanging glaciers on the north faces of Vignemale.

19 Plateau de Saugué, 1644m

A picturesque high plateau with a grand backdrop of the Cirque de Gavarnie

Bareilles – Granges de Saugué – Gîte d'Etape de Saugué and back

Location: Gavarnie, 1360m.
Starting point: Bareilles, 1300m. About 1.5km before Gavarnie a small road branches off to the right and crosses the Gave de Gavarnie. Car park on the right-hand bend before the hamlet.
Walking times: Bareilles – Granges de Saugué 1¼ hrs.; Granges de Saugué – Gîte d'Etape de Saugué ½ hr.; return 1½ hrs.; total time 3¼ hrs.
Difference in height: 344m.
Grade: easy walk on hiking trails and roadways; in places along the GR10.
Refreshments: Gavarnie; Gîte d'Etape de Saugué.
Refuge: Gîte d'Etape de Saugué (15.05.-15.10.); B: 35; ✆ 05.62.92.48.73.

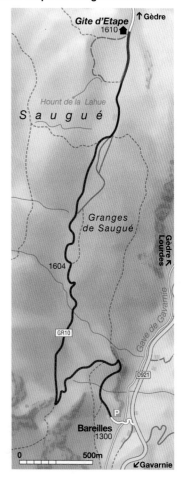

Stylishly renovated old barns, green pastures, meadows of flowers, beehives, and in the background the wide-sweeping rock faces of the Cirque de Gavarnie – the plateau de Saugué is a real feast for the eyes and invites you to linger a while to enjoy the cultivated mountain scenery in front of a dramatic backdrop.

The hiking path begins in **Bareilles** between the first houses of the hamlet where there's a sign for Gîte d'Etape/Granges Saugué. It rapidly ascends up between dry stonewalls, turns off left after about 100m and continues round bends to a track with a sewerage pit. Follow the steady uphill track, past a second pit, to where it ends 50m further on and you continue southwards along a narrow forest path. Following this you meet a cross path after a few minutes which you walk along to the right for a few metres and then continue uphill to the left. The path reaches open ground where there's a view of the Cirque de Gavarnie and now runs directly towards a rock with an electricity pylon. There you join the GR10 which comes up out of the valley of the Gave d'Ossoue.

Follow the signpost marked Saugué to the right and now walk along the idyllic high path across slopes covered in flowers with a pretty view into the valley and over to Montagne de Coumély opposite.

After you have crossed a side-stream the path soon becomes an overgrown roadway which brings you to the sprawling **Granges de Saugué**, 1600m. The roadway runs straight on between the smart barns while the GR10 turns off beforehand and leads along beside the fenced meadows on the left past the Granges.

Continue across the gently rolling meadows of the plateau and you meet the roadway again, then a car park where the road coming up from Gèdre ends. From here it's another few minutes walk along the road to the **Gîte d'Etape**, 1610m, which is an inviting place to take an extended rest.

Plateau de Saugué: idyllic plateau with a backdrop of the cirque.

20 Lac de Cestrède, 1962m, and Lac d'Antarrouyes, 2009m

A delightful high valley at the foot of Cestrède peak

Bué car park – Lac de Cestrède – Lac d'Antarrouyes and back

Location: Gèdre, 1011m.
Starting point: car park at the end of the roadway into Vallée de Cestrède, 1436m. Approach from Gèdre: at the southern end of the village on the hairpin bend go right in the direction of Ayrues, then continue left along a good roadway right up to the end.
Walking times: car park – Lac de Cestrède 2 hrs.; Lac de Cestrède – Lac d'Antarrouyes ½ hr.; return 2¼ hrs.; total time 4¾ hrs.
Difference in height: 573m.
Grade: walk with predominantly steep ascents on obvious paths; short stretches along GR10.
Slightly exposed section of path to Lac d'Antar-rouyes.
Refreshments: Gèdre.

The upper Vallée de Cestrède is a long valley range, enclosed by basin-shaped walls. The idyllic Lac de Cestrède lies at the entrance to the high valley, surrounded by extensive marshlands in which the stream of the same name divides many times. The neighbouring Lac d'Antarroyes lies hidden in a granite basin located higher up.

From the **carpark** you take the path to the left, where, as well as other destinations, Lac de Cestrède is signposted. After a short stretch you meet the GR10 route coming up from Trimbareilles, which you follow to the right. With views of the pretty waterfalls at the end of the valley you climb grassy slopes up the valley until you come to a fork in the path in front of a small forest, where the GR turns off left up to the Plateau de Saugué. Go right along a more or less flat path to a torrent with a cement bridge over it. Immediately after this the path once more splits into two. Again keep to the right and across grassy slopes follow the path, which starts to climb at a noticeable gradient after a small forest and winds up to the broad waterfall. The following series of steep bends brings you to yet another fork (the right path leads to a tunnel in the rock) where you bear left. In a southerly direction go straight across the slope and then a sharp bend takes you up to a ledge. The two outlets from the lake merge at this point and flow into the Cascade

In Val Cestrède.

de Soutarra, above which you have just climbed. Between the confluence of the streams and the waterfall the water vanishes temporarily and returns to the surface 70m further on. You will notice a small weir in the streambed and in front of you, Lac d'Antarrouyes waterfall. Then walk downhill for a while through granite boulders, rhododendrons and ferns as far as the Lac de Cestrède stream. To the left of the wild running stream, climb up the slope over granite, cross the *passerelle* (footbridge) over to the other side until you reach the long-drawn-out plateau and **Lac de Cestrède**, 1962m.

At the end of the lake turn off towards Lac d'Antarrouyes along a meadow path to the right which is indistinct at first, and go round a hilltop, behind which C^{ne} de Cestrède lies hidden. At the hut you take the beaten path in a easterly direction and pass a rain gauge. The path then leads you through small granite hills, slopes down, climbs again briefly and follows a ledge, airy at times, at the edge of steeply dropping slopes. Be very careful on this section of the path when wet! You reach **Lac d'Antarrouyes**, 2009m, near the waterfall where you can get to the other side of the lake via the path along the shore.

21 Refuge des Espuguettes, 2027m, and Pimené, 2801m

A hut in charming surroundings and a superb belvedère

Gavarnie – Refuge des Espuguettes – Col du Pimené – Pimené and back

Location: Gavarnie, 1360m.
Starting point: car park at the entrance to Gavarnie.
Walking times: Gavarnie – Refuge des Espuguettes 2 hrs.; Refuge des Espuguettes – Col du Pimené 1½ hrs; Col du Pimené – Pimené 1 hr; total time 8-8½ hrs.
Difference in height: 1441m.
Grade: broad hiking trail to the Refuge des Espuguettes with a section of steep ascent. From here an obvious path; steep climb to the summit along a narrow ridge with short exposed section and easy

scrambling (I). If there's snow on the summit take special care on the ascent. Altogether a very long walk with a big height variation.
Refreshments: Gavarnie; Refuge des Espuguettes.
Refuge: Refuge des Espuguettes (15.06.-15.09.); B: 60; ℰ 05.62.92.40.63.
Tip: due to the length of the walk, an overnight stay in the refuge is recommended. Standing on the summit at dawn is particularly splendid; you should therefore set out on the walk about 3 hrs. before dawn.
Linking tip: see Walk 11: round walk

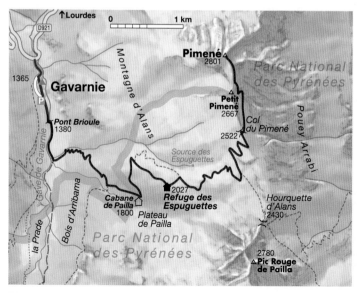

On the way to Pimené with the Refuge des Espuguettes on the right.

through the Cirque de Gavarnie.

Alternative: ascent from the Hourquette d'Alans in the Cirque d'Estaubé, 2430m. On the pass go to the right along the path which at first descends round a few bends then goes down across a long slope to the point where it meets the ascent path from the Refuge des Espuguettes. The climb over the Cirque d'Estaubé rewards you with an unexpected view of the scenery around Gavarnie, but the disadvantage is the descent of just under 200 vertical metres from the pass. Access through the Cirque d'Estaubé, see Walk 25: Hourquette d'Alans.

Tip: if you want to shorten this long hike, the easy walk to the Refuge des Espuguettes makes a quite delightful alternative with wonderful views of the inner Gavarnie area.

Its excellent location in the Cirque de Pailla makes the Refuge des Espuguettes an attractive destination for a hike with a magnificent panoramic view of the landscape. From here you can climb the summit of the Pimené, which is comparatively unstriking, but where F. Schrader, a famous French pioneer of the Pyrenees in the 19th century, made a widely respected sketch of the view – a first class recommendation for the ascent which, together with the Brèche de Roland, is one of the classic walks in the high mountain area of Gavarnie.

In **Gavarnie** you follow the path in Walk 11 at first as far as the fork before the Plateau de Pailla, where you then turn off left to the signposted Refuge des Espuguettes. Climb up to the pretty high meadow, where the massive Rouge de Pailla peak rises in the south-east. Shortly after having passed the national park boundary the path splits into two. Straight on takes you to the C^{ne} de Pailla. The well-trodden dirt path to the left takes you directly to the hill where the hut is located. From here the path then bends abruptly to the north-west in order to go round the steep slope. On a moderate incline the path changes direction again and again, resulting in a constantly varying view of fascinating mountain chains and peaks. Just after the path bends sharply to the south-east in the direction of the refuge, ignore the path off to the left (it skirts round the hut). The path then climbs steeply up to the **Refuge des Espuguettes**, 2027m.

At the refuge take the path that ascends north-eastwards to the signposts where you meet the previous path that offered an alternative route round the hut. Carry on to the right, zigzagging up a comfortable incline, crossing grassy slopes as you gain about 200 vertical metres before reaching the turn-off in the direction of Hourquette d'Alans. The wider slope that goes off diagonally to the right takes you up to the pass into the Cirque d'Estaubé. However go straight on following the sign to 'Petit Pimené'. The long route up the slope to the north comprises of several short bends in the path, which soon straighten out again. Climbing up the incline at times steeply, at times more moderately, you eventually arrive at the **Col du Pimené**, 2522m. Standing high about the Gave d'Estaubé valley you get your first impression of the sheer, towering walls at the end of the valley. Don't take the narrow path waymarked with cairns following the ridge up to Petit Pimené. Cross over to the east side of the ridge and follow the path that flanks the serrated crest in a northerly direction – you can't go wrong if you follow the cairns. The path now takes you over stony ground. Go left on to the rocky slope and zigzag up to the flat ridge and a large cairn. The climb to the summit to the north starts with really steep bends in the path on the relatively wide ridge of Piméné. Some bits of rock jutting out help you to find purchase when climbing up the scree. The ridge then tapers off quite dramatically to a really narrow ridge with a short exposed section. Using your hands on the rock you reach the splendid **Pimené** viewpoint, 2801m. Mont Perdu, Cylindre, Astazous, Marboré, the whole mountain range of the Cirque de Gavarnie, Brèche de Roland, Gabiétous and Vignemale – a unique panorama!

Last stage on the way up to Pimené.

22 Cirque de Lis, 1596m

A secluded side valley with an abrupt end

Pragnères – Pont de Crabiou – Cirque de Lis and back

Location: Gèdre, 1011m.
Starting point: Pragnères, 912m, car park opposite the electricity works. Approach from Gèdre along the D921 in the direction of Luz-St.-Saveur.
Walking times: car park – Pont de Crabiou 1¼ hrs.; Pont de Crabiou –

Cirque de Lis 1 hr.; return 1¾ hrs.; total time 4 hrs.
Difference in height: 684m.
Grade: easy valley walk along good clear paths with a predominantly gentle ascent.
Refreshments: Gèdre.

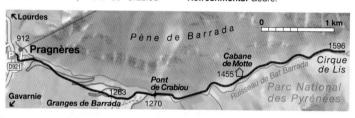

The pretty meadow valley of the wild R^au de Bat Barrada is closed off by the small Cirque de Lis. 'Bat Barrada' in the local language means 'vallée fermé' (closed valley) and the cirque actually forms a type of hermetic seal, which is only broken by the Marraut gorge. At dusk the contrast between the towering circle of mountains and the flat meadow floor scattered with small rivulets is particularly atmospheric.

The signposted footpath begins at the access road between the houses and the stream opposite the **car park**. The path soon crosses the stream over the bridge and continues between dry stone walls and over undulating pastures. At the next fork (left leads to a small bridge) keep to the right until you come to a track which you leave immediately to the left after the narrow right-hand bend (signpost) and enter the forest The wide and shady path quickly begins to climb and crosses a driveway to two small houses, before meeting the track again, which you then follow to the left. Ignoring the downhill path to the right stay on the track for about 500m until you reach a sharp bend to the right, where you head left into forest (signpost). The attractive path through beech, pine and box trees rises quickly above the stream up to open meadows where it meets the R^au de Bat Barrada again. Walking through a beautiful beech forest stay to the right of the stream until the path joins the track again. Go left to **Pont de Crabiou**, 1270m, and on the other side walk upstream across grassy slopes covered in flowers. After a larger hut go past the national park boundary, go through a cattle gate (don't forget to close it after you) and walk alongside the stream through a thin wood. With a clear increase in gradient the path climbs across grassy slopes up to Cⁿᵉ de Motte, but eases up again after passing the shepherds' hut. You approach a narrowing in the valley where the stream has carved a gorge-like channel into the rock. Walk high above the wild stream, through the cleft of the valley after which you cross a wide scree slope which drops down from the left, until you reach the flat valley floor where the numerous water channels that flow down the steep mountainside join to form the valley stream. The path heads for the Gorge de Marraut that cuts through the basin-shaped valley to the north-east. The walk comes to an end in the middle of the **Cirque de Lis**, 1596m.

The view down the valley takes in the mountains of Ardiden.

23 Pic de Bergons, 2068m

Inconspicuous mountain but with a brilliant view

Vallon de l'Yse – Pic de Bergons and back

Location: Luz-St-Sauveur, 700m.
Starting point: end of the track into the Vallon de l'Yse, 1670m.

As you come out of the village of Luz (D918 in the direction of Barèges) turn off along the D146 in the direction of Astes. Go through Villenave and Astes, then the road becomes a good forest track which winds its way across the slopes of the Yse valley.

At a fork quite a way up, continue uphill to the right and park at the side of the road about 50m before the building at the end of the track.

Walking times: car park – Pic de Bergons 1¼ hrs.; return 1 hr.; total time 2¼ hrs.
Difference in height: 398m.
Grade: easy, short walk along gently ascending and winding path.
Refreshments: Luz-St-Sauveur.
Alternative: if you would like to extend the walk across the flowering slopes of the Vallon de l'Yse you can park on a distinct hairpin bend to the left (1442m), shortly before a wooden sign 'Zone pastorale'. The obvious path turns off here and takes a shortcut across the loops of the track to meet up with it again at the top by the car park.

Vallon de l'Yse is straight out of a picture book with its rich meadows, luxuriant hills covered in flowers, splendid barns, and surrounded by impressive rocks and green mountain chains. The unobtrusive stature of Pic de Bergons plays an insignificant role in this landscape, but reaching the vantage point is not as easy and quick as it seems.

At the **car park** follow the dirt path down past a wooden post at the edge of the track, then immediately climb uphill in a south-easterly direction. A bit further up the path bends to the west and heads up and across the long

Vallon d'Yse: a picture-book valley.

slope at a comfortable incline, offering lovely views of the Yse valley, Luz-St-Sauveur and surrounding area. Follow another bend and make another longer climb across the slope, followed by a couple of steep turns, until you reach Portillon de Bachebirou and its *cabane* of the same name. From here the path turns westwards once again and leads along the ridge up to the gentle **Pic de Bergons**, 2068m, which drops abruptly away down to the south and to the west.

24 Col de Pierrefitte, 2466m

Face to face with the Néouvielle peaks

Vallon de l'Yse – Cabane de Peyrahitte – Col de Pierrefitte and back

Location: Luz-St.-Sauveur, 700m.
Starting point: end of the track into the Vallon de l'Yse, 1560m. As you leave the village of Luz (D918 in the direction of Barèges) turn off along the D146 in the direction of Astes. Go through Villenave and Astes, then the road becomes a good forest track. At a fork quite a way up (1540m) you go straight on leisurely downhill to the stream. The track ends at a bridge over the R^{au} de l'Yse and it's possible to park

about 100m before that.
Walking times: car park – C^{ne} de Peyrahitte 1¼ hrs.; C^{ne} de Peyrahitte – Col de Pierrefitte 1½ hrs.; return 2¼ hrs.; total time 5 hrs.
Difference in height: 906m.
Grade: easy valley walk on a broad path as far as the *cabane*; a well-trodden path to the col; now and then some steep ascents.
Refreshments: Luz-St.-Sauveur.

Cabane de Peyrahitte in the attractive upper Yse valley is a favourite destination for a problem-free, peaceful stroll. From here the hiking path climbs up further to the Pierrefitte pass, which forms the entrance into the neighbouring Néouvielle area, and has a magnificent view over the jagged peaks of the 3000ers around Pic de Néouvielle.

From the **car park** head for the bridge and cross over to the other side of the R^{au} de l'Yse, where you pick up the forest path. About 50m before the first house leave the forest path and climb up right along the old roadway in the

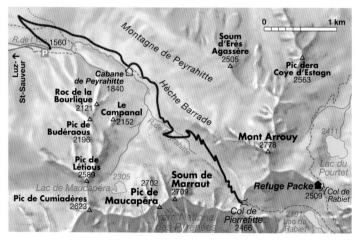

Cabane de Peyrahitte: in the background the sillhouette of the Néouvielle spikes.

Yse valley. This then heads down the valley at first, then makes a sharp turn at the *cabane* and runs up a moderate incline into the valley. With a view of the steep Soum de Marraut and Pic de Maucapé summits in the south-west, walk across hillside pastures towards the hut which lies on a flat-topped grassy hill above the waterfall of the valley stream. Just before the hut, the path ascends a little and arrives at the **C^{ne} de Peyrahitte**, 1840m. Several foundation walls around the hut date from the building of a water conduit between Lac de Cap de Long in the Néouvielle and Pragnères electricity works at Gèdre.

From the *cabane* the roadway goes round a bend over to the left-hand slope where there's a good view of the path up to the Col de Pierrefitte. It climbs leisurely up the slope on a lengthy diagonal and on the other side of the valley below the Soum de Marraut you can see a rock 'window', part of the conduit system.

The valley gets narrower and the path now leads more steeply uphill as far as a grassy ledge with a fork. The narrow path to the right leads to Lac de Maucapéra, but you continue left in accordance with the signpost and immediately cross over the streambed to follow the long-drawn-out bends on the left-hand slope. The col lies ahead with the twin peaks of Mont Arrouy. At a gentler incline you gain some height and come to a large area of scree which you cross over. The broad and well-levelled path is waymarked with cairns. It winds its way through the multi-coloured rock and then becomes a loose path up the hill where the gradient increases a little before reaching the **Col de Pierrefitte**, 2466m.

25 Through the Cirque d'Estaubé to the Hourquette d'Alans, 2430m

A quiet walk with superb scenery

Lac des Gloriettes – national park boundary – Hourquette d'Alans and back

Location: Gèdre, 1011m.
Starting point: car park at Lac des Gloriettes, 1650m. Approach from Gèdre on the D922 in the direction of Troumouse-Héas; at the Pont de l'Arraillé turn off right along the D176 to the reservoir (closed off in winter).
Walking times: car park – national park boundary 1¼ hrs.; national park boundary – Hourquette d'Alans 1¾ hrs.; return 2½ hrs.; total time 5½ hrs.
Difference in height: 780m.
Grade: long, but not a difficult walk technically on HRP; mostly gently ascending track, but steeper on the slope to the pass. Some waymarkers.
Refreshments: Gèdre;
Alternative: Pla d'Ailhet, 1800m, at the end of the Cirque d'Estaubé. Totally effortless stroll as far as the impressive head of the valley with the prominent cleft of Brèche de Tuquerouye, across which Louis Ramond, early explorer of the Pyrenees, undertook his exploratory expedition for the ascent of Monte Perdido 200 years ago.

At the fork in the path beyond the national park boundary follow the signpost for the Cabane d'Estaubé. Go left to the stream and cross over to the other side on the bridge. The path continues up the valley again, ascends a little way, passes the Cabane d'Estaubé and then follows the stream without significant incline as far as the Pla d'Ailhet, 1800m. Total time 3¼ hrs.
Linking tip: see Walk 21.

The Estaubé valley is closed off by sheer rock walls.

The Cirque d'Estaubé cannot compete with the imposing dimensions of the Cirque de Gavarnie or Cirque de Troumouse. However it is the modest scale, the peacefulness and the wonderful landscape of the valley that gives it a particular charm. The climb up to the Hourquette d'Alans in the area to the west of the head of the valley rewards you with magnificent views of the mountains of Gavarnie. Fit mountain walkers can also add on the brilliant walk to Pimené.

Cross over the reservoir dam of the **Lac des Gloriettes** and follow the signpost to Hourquette d'Alans. Walk along the shore to the southern end of the lake where you start across the valley plain of the Gave d'Estaubé at a fence with a gate. The upper sections of the cirque walls are already emerging at the head of the valley. The path now runs alongside the crystal clear stream through the charming valley as far as the national park boundary after which there's a fork (see alternative).

With your objective being the Hourquette d'Alans, keep going straight ahead. The path ascends the slope and after a bend reaches a ledge with a splendid view of the

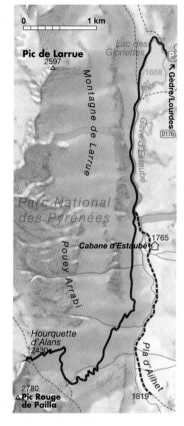

cirque and the valley floor. It then continues up a pleasant incline. After crossing a stream it zigzags uphill, heading in the direction of the strikingly formed Pic Rouge de Pailla. The rock buttress drops down on the right to the Hourquette d'Alans.

Go past a path turning off left to the Brèche du Tuquerouye and cross the hillside to the north, then with a conspicuous change in direction climb up the winding and stony path to the west towards the top of the pass. Another ascent just before the pass brings you up to the **Hourquette d'Alans**, 2430m.

26 Cirque de Troumouse, 2138m

Pastoral idyll in an impressive glacier basin

Chapelle de Héas – Cabane des Aires – Lacs des Aires – le Cot and back

Location: Gèdre, 1011m.
Starting point: car park just behind the Chapelle de Héas (about 100m before the pay station for the pass road into the Cirque), 1520m.
Approach from Gèdre on the D922 in the direction of Troumouse-Héas (closed off in winter).

Walking times: car park – Lacs des Aires 1¾ hrs.; Lacs des Aires – le Cot ½ hr.; return 2 hrs.; total time 4¼ hrs.
Difference in height: 618m.
Grade: technically easy walk on good hiking paths, although a short steep ascent up a slope in between.
Refreshments: Gèdre.

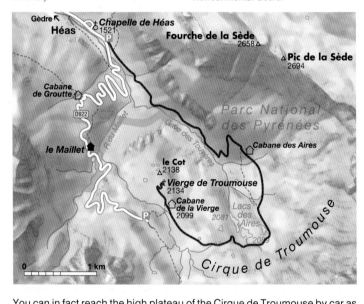

You can in fact reach the high plateau of the Cirque de Troumouse by car as well, but the fabulous backdrop of the mountain basin shaped by glaciers is revealed far more strikingly along the hiking path beside the Gave des Touyères. Particularly eye-catching is the contrast between the almost flat pastures with their shallow lakes and the abruptly rising rock walls of the Cirque.

Historic photo by Lucien Briet at the Cirque de Troumousse (1895).

The central point, and at the same time the highest peak of the stone amphitheater, is Pico de la Munia at 3134m.

The sign-posted hiking path (Cirque de Troumouse / Lacs des Aires) begins at the **car park** and immediately passes a turn-off left to Hourquette de Héas. Continuing straight on you rapidly ascend across the grassy slopes above the regulated Gave des Touyères and enter the national park at a border sign. After a level stretch the path begins to ascend again and after several rivulets zigzags steeply uphill, quickly gaining height. The imposing backdrop of the Cirque de Troumouse comes gradually into view as you ascend the hillside. Climb up as far as the fork just before you reach some ledges on the slope. A direct path continues straight ahead to the Cirque de Troumouse, while a detour branches off left to the C^{ne} des Aires, which allows you a more beautiful view across the high plateau. The ¼ hour detour brings you to the **Cabane des Aires**, 2132m, from where several paths make their way towards the head of the valley. You soon join the main path again, which you follow through pleasant pastureland, and arrive at the shallow **Lacs des Aires**, 2099m.

Walk round the lakes on the south side. Heading west, the path now leads out of the Cirque, passes a rain gauge and then keeps along beside the pretty meandering R^{au} de Cot. The statue of Mary on the hill ahead is already in sight. At the following fork take the path turning off right sign-posted to Vierge de Troumouse, walk past the C^{ne} de la Vierge and climb up onto the hilltop of **le Cot**, 2138m.

The Pics de Gerbats, Troumouse, la Munia and Pène Blanque stand out most prominently as you cast your gaze over the large circle of mountains from east to west.

27 Hourquette de Héas, 2608m, and Hourquette de Chermentas, 2439m

In the easternmost corner of the Parc National des Pyrénées

Piau-Engaly ski station – turn-off to Port de Campbieil – Hourquette de Héas – Hourquette de Chermentas and back

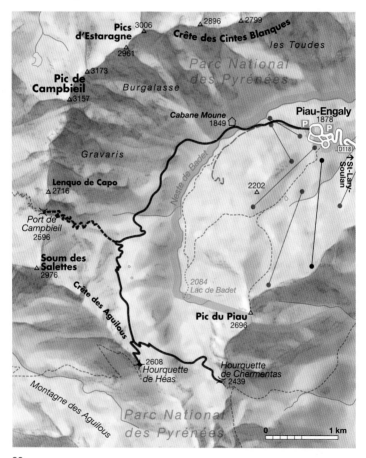

At your destination: Hourquette de Chermentas with the Spanish border mountains.

Location: Fabian, 1140m.

Starting point: car park at Piau-Engaly ski station, 1878m. Approach from Fabian on the D118 as far as the ski station. (Follow signs for P-Journée.)

Walking times: car park – turn-off to Port de Campbieil 1¼ hrs.; turn-off to Port de Campbieil – Hourquette de Héas 1½ hrs.; Hourquette de Héas – Hourquette de Chermentas ¾ hr.; return 2½ hrs.; total time 6 hrs.

Difference in height: 730m.

Grade: long walk without any technical difficulties on good paths; several steeper inclines.

The ascent of the steep slope to the Hourquette de Héas pass is dangerous in compact snow!

Refreshments: Fabian.

Alternative: Port de Campbieil, 2596m. Interesting pass with views between dramatically formed rock walls. The whole path is well marked with cairns.

At the fork to Port de Campbieil (way-marker boards a large pile of stones) turn off in a north westerly direction, at first leisurely ascending across level stony slopes with large loose stones. The path soon winds up the scree slope, becomes a steep incline and then for the rest of the way keeps on the right of the scree coming down from the col. The top of the pass is always in sight and just below it the path gets even steeper again and you quickly reach Port de Campbieil (sign and cairn). There and back 1½ h.

Meadows of flowers, marmots, chamoix and birds of prey are your companions on this pleasant walk through the Neste de Badet valley up to two narrow clefts forming hidden passes which give you wonderful views of the varied landscape. While the Hourquette de Héas opens up the view of an enchanting valley to the west in the direction of Héas, the dramatic formations of the nearby Spanish mountains can be seen on the Hourquette de Chermentas. Even if you are satisfied with only one of these ascents up to a pass, you will still enjoy a walk with beautiful scenery in a quiet corner of the national park.

At **Piau-Engaly ski station** walk past two lift buildings and shortly afterwards at the signpost for Port de Campbieil set off along the hiking path. This soon branches off from the track, follows the Neste and then changes over onto the other bank of the stream on a bridge. Signs indicate the entrance into the area of the national park. Keep on the right-hand bank of the Neste at first, past the Cⁿᵉ de Moune, and gradually move away from the course of the stream. First of all the path keeps to the foot of the steep slope, then traverses the hillside at a pleasant gradient, but soon afterwards, leads up the hillside more steeply. The valley is dominated by the Crête de Cintes Blanques whose striking rock formations display a lively array of colours when the light is favourable.

After a rapid ascent the path levels out noticeably and runs across the grassy slopes to a little bridge. Cross the stream here and 100m afterwards you come to a junction with a sign where Lac de Badet is indicated to the left and Port de Campbieil to the right. Keep to the right and climb above the stream to a level widening of the valley where you arrive at the **turn-off for Port de Campbieil**, 2225m. Signposts by a large pile of stones show the way for the ascent up to Port de Campbieil (see alternative), but you take the direction of Hourquette de Héas / Hourquette de Chermentas and ascend to the south round gentle bends across sloping pastures. You quickly reach a more level section of the hillside across which the path now runs below the Crête de Aguilous as far as a large cairn at the foot of a long scree slope. Turn off here to the right and after a few minutes you meet another sign-posted fork where you keep straight ahead to climb up along the narrow stony path across the steep scree slopes. The path winds up to a prominent rocky bank and continues there on a broad band of rock which leads to the **Hourquette de Héas**, 2608m. The view from the top of the pass is stunning; famous peaks in the south-west like Monte Perdido, Vignemale, Balaïtous and the mountain tops of the Cirque de Gavarnie, in the north the mountains of Vallée d'Aure and to the west you can see a pretty valley dropping down to Héas.

Descend the steep slope again to the last fork, turn there to the right and meet the path further below which runs at first on the level then descends for a lengthy stretch, as it heads towards the basin-shaped head of the valley. The path changes over to the other hillside, climbs up across pastures and eventually winds up the narrow hollow of the col to **Hourquette de Chermentas**, 2439m. The view reaches far into the Spanish mountains as far as Punta Suelza.

Fog at Hourquette de Héas.

28 Lacs and Refuge de Barroude, 2355m

Two picturesque lakes at the foot of a wonderful rock buttress

Aragnouet-le Plan – Cabanes de la Géla – Lacs de Barroude and back

Location: Fabian, 1140m.
Starting point: forest track on the D173, 1390m. Approach from Fabian on the D118, past the turn-off to le Plan and Piau-Engaly as far as the first hairpin bend with a small parking place at the side of the road.
Walking times: car park – Cabanes de la Géla 1 hr.; Cabanes de la Géla – Lacs de Barroude 1¾ hrs.; return 2½ hrs.; total time 5¼ hrs.
Difference in height: 965m.
Grade: easy walk on roadways and walking paths; a really steep incline in the middle section.
Refreshments: Fabian; Refuge de Barroude.
Refuge: Refuge de Barroude (15.06.-15.09); B:20 ✆ 05.62.39.61.10.
Alternative: Port de Barroude, 2535m. The border pass to the Spanish Circo de Barrosa is reached in a good half an hour's easy ascent. At the southern end of the big lake you continue to follow the hiking path; it ascends gently at first, then swings onto the slope of the col and winds up round short bends to the broad pass. There and back from the Refuge de Barroude 1¼ hrs.

The Muraille de Barroude is an imposing rock wall which swings steeply up to its 500m and the high plateau marks the boundary between the lakes and the adjacent western Cirque de Troumouse. The highest point of the buttress is the prominent Pic de Troumouse, on whose northern slopes a tiny remaining glacier clings. Both lakes fit beautifully into the dramatic backdrop of rocks.

From the **car park** go a few steps up the road and turn onto the forest track branching off to the right. Walk up the valley along the Neste on an old path where they used to transport the lead, silver and zinc which was mined at Port Vieux. After a signpost (Refuge de Barroude) the roadway ascends steeply and gets narrower. Way below you can see the stream plunging through a pretty section of the gorge and there's a safety handrail at the edge of the precipitous hillside. A short stretch runs through forest after which a sign 'Attention. Chute de Pierres' warns you of rock fall at the foot of a steep scree slope. Again through forest, you move toward the less lively stream and continue at the same level. Pass a cattle gate (remember to close it after you) and enter the high valley with lush green meadows. The path forks here. Left is sign-posted to Port Vieux Espagne and your destination of Barroude is indicated across a little wooden bridge to the other side of the stream where the national park immediately begins. The now narrow path keeps by the stream for a while longer and crosses the pleasant pastures of the widening valley. Pass by the **Cabanes de la Géla**, 1705m, on the other side of the Neste, keep in the valley bottom for a short way and then begin a slowly ascending traverse across the slope after which the path becomes a broad grassy ledge. It leads round long bends up the slope in the direction of the broad rock face, Pichous de Barroude, which is eroded by several waterfalls. Keep left at a junction along the now steeply rising path. As it turns briefly to the north, then back to the west, the gradient slackens off again and you head towards the outstanding Muraille de Barroude.

The signpost at the fork indicates right to Hourquette de Chermentas, but you turn left and walk past scattered boulders and tiny pools in the shade of the fabulous rock buttress to the end of the high plateau with the magnificent sprawling **Lac de Barroude**, 2355m. The **Refuge de Barroude**, 2377m, stands a little higher up on the left of the path behind which the smaller of the two lakes lies hidden.

In front of a spectacular backdrop: Lacs de Barroude and refuge.

29 Pic de Campbieil, 3173m

Fabulous views from a 3000er

Lac de Cap de Long – Pic de Campbieil and back

Location: Fabian, 1140m.
Starting point: car park at Lac de Cap de Long, 2175m. Approach from Fabian on the D929 as far as the car park at the lake.
Walking times: Lac de Cap de Long – Pic de Campbieil 3½ hrs.; return 3 hrs.; total time 6½ hrs.
Difference in height: 998m.
Grade: long high mountain walk with a respectable variation in height; the paths are really steep in places and the summit as-

cent is loose and very steep. Walking poles are recommended. Cairns.
Refreshments: Fabian; bar at Lac de Cap de Long (in summer).
Tip: on the IGN Néouvielle map (1748 ET) Pic de Campbieil is marked 'Pic de Campbieil ou Pic Badet' as a subsidiary peak of Pic Long.
The peak described here, on the other hand, is marked 'Pic Badet ou Pic de Campbieil'.

The kidney-shaped Lac de Cap de Long, the largest lake in the Néouvielle area, is the starting point for this walk onto a brilliant summit for views and which is never overrun, even in summer. Together with the huge mountain chains and peaks that can be seen all around, the lively contrasts in scenery as you make the ascent, make for an exciting and powerful mountain experience.

Begin the walk at **Lac de Cap de Long** along the southern end of the lake. The road quickly becomes a shore side path where there has been a large rock fall. Find your way through the boulders and afterwards the path branches off on an ascending traverse of the hillside until it turns directly onto the slope and winds its way quickly up round some very steep bends at times and gains height above the lake.

Then follows a lengthy traverse with several ascents in between. The path levels out as you head towards the western end of the lake. The path turns to the south into the valley of the R^{au} de Cap de Long – you keep on the lower path – and runs up between the large granite slope on the left and a small rounded hilltop at whose left edge you ascend to a platform. You now come closer

A spectacle of peaks on the Pic de Campbiell: on the right Monte Perdido with glacier.

to the valley stream, change over to the other side at a cairn and head towards the steep start of the slope, which the stream runs through. The path winds really strenuously and at times steeply up to a pink-coloured granite hump which you either climb over or go round to the right. Both paths meet up again in a pretty little high valley with a tiny lake. The path crosses over the stream and climbs up the slope again.

Leaving the granite rock you come to an area of slate. Gradually the grassy vegetation recedes completely and you are walking over bare rock where tiny enclaves of flowers have taken hold. The uncommonly colourful rocky landscape keeps drawing your attention and in the west you can see Pic Long with a small remaining glacier. The peak you are aiming for stands out in the south due to its striking brown colour. The path along beside the cairns heads for the long-drawn-out col and beyond it lies Gourg de Cap de Long, a lake which receives the water of the small basin. The path turns off left on the col, heads towards your objective and then turns onto the broad scree slope which drops down from the ridge of the Pic. Going at first up some zigzags, a long steep traverse brings you to some more bends and the path ascends to the ridge that you must now follow to the left to reach **Pic de Campbieil**, 3173m.

A staggering spectacle of peaks from Pico de Aneto in the east to Vignemale in the west, not to mention the surrounding crests and peaks of Néouvielle!

30 Hourquette d'Aubert, 2498m

Superb views across the big lakes of the Néouvielle national park

Lac d'Aubert – Hourquette d'Aubert and back

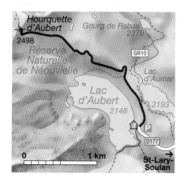

Location: Fabian, 1140m.
Starting point: car park at Lac d'Aubert, 2168m. Approach from Fabian on the D929, then turn off in the direction of Lac d'Orédon onto the D177.
Walking times: Lac d'Aubert – Hourquette d'Aubert 1 hr.; return ¾ hr.; total time 1¾ hrs.
Difference in height: 300m.
Grade: undemanding, short walk on a well-made path.
Refreshments: Fabian; Refuge Hôtel d'Orédon on Lac d'Orédon.
Tip: controlled access to Lac d'Aubert: see p. 11.

Néouvielle national park.

At Hourquette d'Aubert: view of the Lacs d'Aubert and d'Aumar.

There's a striking view from the top of the pass across Lac d'Aubert of the beautiful landscape of lakes in the national park and the granite chain with the conspicuous Pic de Néouvielle and its small remaining glaciers. If the light is good Pic du Midi de Bigorre also stands out prominently in the north, easily recognizable from the observatory and the large antenna on the summit.

From **Lac d'Aubert** take the path sign-posted to Hourquette d'Aubert. Between Lac d'Aubert and Lac d'Aumar walk through a delightful 'garden of rocks' with rhododendron, very old pine trees and clearings covered in flowers.

Keep left at the turn-off with the signpost to the Col de Madaméte. The col can already to be clearly seen ahead in the west towards which the path now ascends. A small rocky balcony offers a pretty view back of the lakes, and then the path gets a little steeper and runs across flat slabs of granite. After a longish stretch of 'paved' path you start to cross the slope at a steady and leisurely incline in the direction of the col. Some bends still await you at the end of the traverse and then you arrive at **Hourquette d'Aubert**, 2498m.

31 Long round walk in the Néouvielle area

Lengthy and scenically very varied round walk

Lac d'Aubert – Hourquette d'Aubert – Lac dets Coubous – Cabane d'Aygues Cluses – Col de Madaméte – Lac d'Aubert

Location: Fabian, 1140m.

Starting point: car park at Lac d'Aubert, 2168m. Approach from Fabian on the D929, then turn off in the direction of Lac d'Orédon onto the D177.

Walking times: Lac d'Aubert – Hourquette d'Aubert 1hr.; Hourquette d'Aubert – Lac dets Coubous 1¼ hrs.; Lac dets Coubous – Cabane d'Aygues Cluses 2 hrs.; Cabane d'Aygues Cluses – Col de Madaméte 1½ hrs.; Col de Madaméte – Lac d'Aubert ¾ hr.; total time 6½ hrs.

Difference in height: 1068m (with some ascents in between).

Grade: strenuous and substantial walk with some sections of quite steep ascents and descents in places.

Well-laid walking paths; along the GR10 in the second part of the round walk (through the Aygues-Cluses valley and across the Col de Madaméte to Lac d'Aubert).

Refreshments: Fabian; Refuge Hôtel d'Orédon on Lac d'Orédon.

Tip: controlled access to Lac d'Aubert: see p. 11. (Tourist tips/access).

Alternative: you can also start the round walk at the Jardin botanique on the D918 west of the Col de Tourmalet.

Go up the valley of the Rau Dets Coubous along the GR10 as far as the fork. Additional walking time about ¾ hr.

Countless lakes adorn the Néouvielle region.

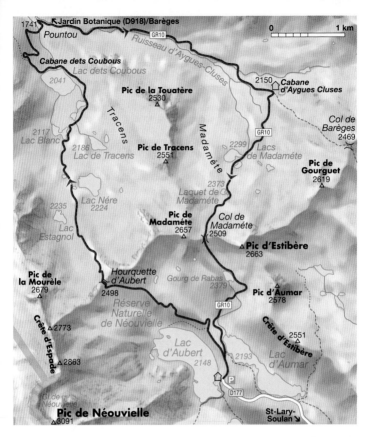

This day walk connects a good dozen or so large and small lakes. They lie in three wide valley basins which are separated by a series of striking ridges. The demanding Parcours offers you an overview of the scenic diversity that characterizes the central area of the Néouvielle national park and adjoining northern region.

From **Lac d'Aubert** you start by following the path in Walk 30 to the **Hourquette d'Aubert**, 2498m. The path continues on the other side of the pass across the hillside at the foot of the rock wall. At first in a straight line, then zigzagging round bends, it quickly descends down into the valley

Col de Madaméte.

where several lakes are to found one after the other. There are plenty of waymarkers on stones to guide you across rocky sections. Alternatively on the level and down a gentle descent you walk through the pretty valley with its small lakes and pools. After you have gone round a dry lake on the right, continue down to **Lac dets Coubous**, 2041m, which is a popular place for fishermen. Go across the dam to the C^{ne} dets Coubous and there take the twisting path down to the valley stream. The steep descent down the eroded slope brings you to a bridge over the stream and on the other side you come directly to the GR10 which comes up from the Jardin botanique along the D918.

Now follow the signpost for the 'Cabane d'Aygues Cluses / Col de Madaméte' and turn into the valley coming down from the right. The path keeps along the stream, the gradient slowly gets steeper and after a fence you come to a fork where you follow the white and red waymarked GR. A delightful plateau stretches out ahead with a meandering stream. As you walk through the pretty little valley you cross many streams and then the steep ascent begins again leading you along the left-hand side of the stream. The path crosses the stream yet again before a dry lake and reaches the **Cabane d'Aygues Cluses**, 2150m, on a wide plateau of pastureland with several lakes.

At the hut follow the signpost pointing south to the Col de Madaméte across

The last stage just before returning to the starting point: Lac d'Aumar.

flat pastures at first, then over hillsides covered in rhododendrons, little rippling streams and numerous small lakes. Ascend through this picturesque landscape where unclear tracks over rock and boulders are usually waymarked with GR signs. After a steeper section of path you cross the stream, come to a terrace on the slope where Lacs de Madaméte are situated and follow the signpost to the Col de Madaméte. The level path runs between two lakes, then gently ascends to another level on the slope with the smaller Laquet de Madaméte and heads towards the obvious cleft of the pass between Pic de Madaméte in the west and Pic d'Estibère in the east. A steep section of the slope brings you to a small lake below the col and a little later you reach the **Col de Madaméte**, 2509m.

The last stage now leads between a long scree slope on your left and a grassy slope on the right covered in boulders and rhododendrons. At a lake you take the path along its left-hand shore over rocks and boulders (be careful). Walk below a very beautifully marked rock face on the left and then, changing direction, the path quickly descends the slope down to the large lakes. Once you have arrived at the plateau with the lakes you walk through meadows to Lac d'Aumar and along the shore to a fork with a sign where you take the path back to the starting point.

32 Stroll round Lac de l'Oule, 1820m

A walk into the Néouvielle region to put you into the mood

Artigusse car park – Lac de l'Oule and back

Location: Fabian, 1130m.
Starting point: Artigusse car park, 1590m. Approach from Fabian (D929).
Walking times: car park – Lac de l'Oule 1 hr.; round the lake 1¼ hrs.; return ¾ hrs.; total time 3 hrs.

Difference in height: 230m.
Grade: easy walk on comfortable walking paths; partly GR10.
Refreshments: Fabian; Refuge de l'Oule.
Refuge: Refuge de l'Oule (1.06.-15.09.); B: 26 ℰ 05.62.98.48.62.

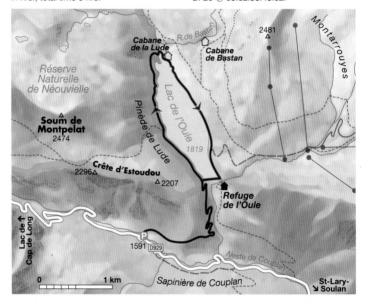

Lac de l'Oule on the boundary of the Réserve Naturelle de Néouvielle is not only a favourite destination for fisherman. Many come here to stroll along the lakeside or to find pretty picnic spots – a particularly pleasant thing to do in the evening.

At the **car park** take the broad roadway which was once used when they were constructing the dam. The path is at first hewn into the steep rock and the embankment falls steeply away on the right. It continues up a gentle incline, leads into a mixed forest of whitebeam, aspens, birch trees and

Lac de l'Oule: a favourite lake for a stroll.

mountain ash and finally goes round easy-angled bends. The forest gradually thins out and you head towards the dam and reach **Lac de l'Oule**, 1820m.

Now continue along the GR path on the left bank for a few metres above the lake. Red spruce, uncinate pine and rhododendron cover the slopes. Ignore the turn-off left to the Col d'Estoudou along the level dirt path and walk to the end of the lake across open meadows which are strewn with boulders. Pass a small hut with a wall around it and immediately afterwards you cross a bridge over the inflow of the stream and arrive at the C^{ne} de la Lude. On the slopes opposite you can still see the old quarries from where the materials for the buildings and dam came. Ignore the path branching off left to Lacs de Bastan (see Walk 33) and return on the eastern side of the lake as far as the ski lift and the Refuge de l'Oule. Cross over the dam to reach your ascent path.

33 Lacs de Bastan, 2260m

Lakes set in a picture book landscape

Artigusse car park – Lac de l'Oule – Lac de Bastan Inférieur – Refuge de Bastan – Lac de Bastan Supérieur and back

Location: Fabian, 1130m.
Starting point: Artigusse car park, 1590m. Approach from Fabian (D929).
Walking times: car park – Lac de l'Oule 1 hr.; Lac de l'Oule – Lac de Bastan Inférieur 1 hrs; Lac de Bastan Inférieur – Refuge de Bastan ¾ hr.; Refuge de Bastan – Lac de Bastan Supérieur ¼ hr.; return 2½ hrs.; total time 5½ hrs.
Difference in height: 670m.
Grade: long, but technically easy walk on

well-laid hiking paths (GR10C alternative); a section of steep ascent in the middle part.
Refreshments: Fabian; Ref. de Bastan.
Refuge: Refuge de Bastan (1.06.-30.09); B: 20 ✆ 05.62.98.48.80.
Tip: you can also walk to Lacs de Bastan along the GR10 from the Col de Portet. See Walk 34: Col de Bastanet and Pic de Bastan.
Linking tip: see Walk 34.

On the way to Lacs de Bastan.

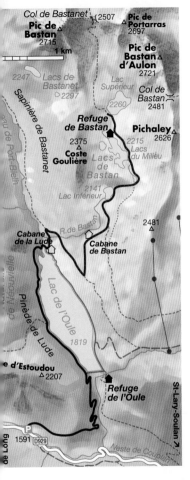

This walk is part of the long north-south crossing in the eastern region of the Néouvielle, where countless mountain lakes are connected to each other. Clear streams, luxuriant rhododendrons, enchanting lakes and the splendid backdrop of the Néouvielle massif in the west characterize the landscape on this varied walk.

The start of this walk follows Walk No. 32 at first. Climb up from the **car park** to Lac de l'Oule and continue as far as the sign-posted fork after the bridge over the stream. Turn off there in the direction of Lacs de Bastan along the now narrow path. It immediately climbs up to a fork, and from here continues right along the white and red marked GR variant. With a rapid incline it runs above the lake in a southerly direction and after a section through a wood it turns sharply away to the north. As you climb the hillsides you come past the C^ne de Bastan and meet the GR10, which leads over from the Col de Portet. Now continue ascending left across the grassy slopes until you reach the delightful **Lac de Bastan Inférieur**, 2140m. Walk round the right-hand shore of the lake and then follow the mostly dry streambed to a higher pool. The path stays on the right of a marshy plain, gradually ascends the elongated Lac de Bastan Milieu, briefly touches the lake shore and after a short climb reaches the **Refuge de Bastan**, 2250m, in its pretty location. The GR leads past the hut to the north and in a few minutes arrives at **Lac de Bastan Supérieur**, 2260m.

34 Col de Bastanet, 2507m, and Pic de Bastan, 2715m

Superb viewpoint amidst the Néouvielle lakes

Col de Portet – Refuge de Bastan – Col de Bastanet – Pic de Bastan and back

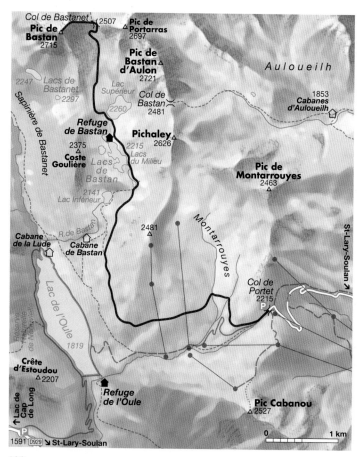

Pic de Bastan with the gently rising Col de Bastanet on the right.

Location: St-Lary-Soulan, 806m.
Starting point: Col de Portet, 2215m. Approach from St-Lary on the D123 in the direction of Espiaube. Just before the ski station turn onto the road to the pass branching off right (track in parts) for 8km up to the Col, where the car park is situated. The road is open from 1.06.-30.09.
Walking times: Col de Portet – Refuge de Bastan 1¾ hrs.; Refuge de Bastan – Col de Bastanet ¾ hr.; Col de Bastanet – Pic de Bastan ½ hr.; return 2½ hrs.; total time 5½ hrs.
Difference in height: 500m.
Grade: an easy walk on the GR10 and GR10C to the Col de Bastanet; steep

climb to Pic de Bastan with short passages of slight exposure; a bit of scrambling below the summit.
Refreshments: St-Lary; Refuge de Bastan.
Refuge: Refuge de Bastan (1.06.-30.09); B: 20 ✆ 05.62.98.48.80.
Alternative: you can extend the walk if you want to by following the GR10C at the Col de Bastan to the numerous lakes situated at varying levels in the north. Refuge de Campana de Cloutou lies at Lac du Campana (1.06.-30.09.) B: 25 ✆ 05.62.91.87.47. Forty five mins. from the Col de Bastanet.
Linking tip: see Walk 33: Lacs de Bastan.

Col de Bastanet.

The Col de Bastanet divides the long chain of lakes in the eastern Néouvielle into Lacs de Bastan in the south and the glittering array of small and big lakes located at varying heights on the north side of the pass. From the pass there are marvellous views of the Réserve Naturelle du Néouvielle and on the narrow summit of the pointed Pic de Bastan the national park lies at your feet.

At the **Col de Portet** take the track going south-west as far as a fork where the hiking path begins. Turning to the west it runs with a slight gradient across meadowed slopes over to Lac de l'Oule, where it turns off to the north and runs almost horizontally for 200m above the big reservoir. At a fork in the path keep straight ahead and a cairn marks a junction where you leave the GR temporarily to the right. The GR path descends a little to the left and meets the path coming up from Lac de l'Oule (see Walk 33: Lacs de Bastan) and then continues to ascend to Lac de Bastan Inférieur. If you want to, you can take this alternative instead as both paths join up again at the small pond above Lac Inférieur. So stay on the level track which later crosses hilly terrain and then joins up again with the GR. Go round the shallow lake on the right, then gently ascend to Lac du Milieu, above which you can already make out the refuge. After a short climb up the slope you reach **Refuge de Bastan**, 2250m. From here continue to the nearby Lac de Bastan Supérieur, which the path only touches briefly to then immediately turn away again. Keep right at a fork on the way and climb up through granite rock, grassy slopes and alpine roses. At the following level area you have a clear view on the left of the gently rising col and Pic de Bastan. Up a moderate incline you now head towards the col, pass the tip of a band of scree and arrive at the hillside to the col. From here you cross a scree slope and climb steeply up on a stony path to the **Col de Bastanet**, 2507m.

The path to Pic de Bastan leaves the col to the west, at first keeping on the left of the rocky crest, but then turns off right, waymarked with cairns, and quickly ascends to the ridge. (The continuing path straight ahead, and possibly the more obvious path, is really steep and loose!) Walk a little way along the ridge and then the path swings to the right of the fissured ridge onto the slope, ascends there and some prominent cairns guide you back onto the ridge with an unforgiving rocky crest beyond. Change over before this onto the left-hand side as the right-hand path is exposed. Both paths meet up again later at the top where the path now becomes really steep and goes over rock. After a kind of cleft you have to descend again for a few metres, then turn immediately sharp left up a steep ascent with a bit of scrambling to **Pic de Bastan**, 2715m, where there's a big summit sign and a fabulous panorama.

Spectacular summit views from Pic de Bastan.

35 Lac de Bareilles, 1765m, and Mont Né, 2147m

A hidden lake and a surprising panoramic peak

Bergerie d'Artigue-Longue – Lac de Bareilles – Mont Né and back

Location: Arreau, 709m.
Starting point: forest track at the Bergerie d'Artigue-Longue, 1510m.
Approach from Arreau on the D112 to Bareilles; about 500m beyond the village take the forest track turning off right at a lay-by in the direction of Lac de Bareilles. After ignoring two tracks branching off to the right and after about 4.8km you can park by a cattle gate at the side of the track.
Walking times: Bergerie d'Artigue-Longue – Lac de Bareilles ¾ hr.; Lac de Bareilles – Mont Né 1½ hrs.; return 1¾ hrs.; total time 4 hrs.
Difference in height: 637m.
Grade: easy walk on yellow marked hiking path; however some sections of steep ascent.
Refreshments: Arreau.
Alternative: Pic du Lion, 2102m. You can extend the return path into a beautiful and easy ridge walk to Pic du Lion.
From the Col de Pierrefite continue to the south on the Crête de Techouède, then in a south-westerly direction along the Crête de la Coume du Lion as far as Pic du Lion with a large cairn.
From there descend the steep slope of the col to the Col de Lion and go northwards along the GRP to the ascent path near Lac de Bareilles. An additional 2 hrs.

Tip: Lac de Bareilles is also marked on the IGN map 1848 OT as 'Lac de Bordères'.

There are stunning views not only from large peaks and sometimes even the ill-defined 2000ers offer brilliant views because of their open position. Mont Né in the green valley of Lac de Bareilles is one of these and is not a mountain in the real sense, rather the highest projection in a long line of ridges, from which you can take in the wonderful massifs of the Central Pyrenees.

At the forest track near to the **Bergerie d'Artigue-Longue** follow the sign-post for Lac de Bordères along the grassy track to the south. It heads towards a huge pine tree, beyond which the track divides about 100m later. Following the yellow waymarkers, continue to the right and ascend idyllic pastures to a little pine forest which you quickly walk through. While the valley stream cascades down over ledges in small waterfalls on the left below, climb steeply up the hillside and come to another little wood and after that go uphill across slopes covered in alpine roses to **Lac de Bareilles**, 1765m. The quiet lake lies in a small valley basin created by a series of ridges. Go left beside the lake, over the outflowing stream and continue along a level path until you meet the GRP 'Tour Oueil-Larboust' which you take to the left. Turning to the north-east start up the gentle ascent to Port de Pierrefite (1855m), which is waymarked by a circle of stones with a rock pillar in the middle.

The path to Pic de Lion (see alternative) is sign-posted to the south while to the north you continue to Mont Né. Leave the GRP here which descends into Vallée d'Oueil, and climb up beside the cattle fence along the at first broad crest of the ridge. It immediately gets narrower and drops steeply down to the right. After a long strenuous climb the path levels out again somewhat and reaches the rounded summit of **Mont Né**, 2147m, with geodetic sign and wooden post.

The stone circle with the rock pillar at Port de Pierrefite.

36 Lac d'Oô, 1504m, and Refuge d'Espingo, 1950m

A lake popular with daytrippers with idyllic high mountain scenery above

Granges d'Astau – Lac d'Oô – Refuge d'Espingo and back

Location: Oô, 968m.
Starting point: car park at the Granges d'Astau at the end of the D76 into the Val d'Astau, 1139m.
Walking times: Granges d'Astau – Lac d'Oô 1¼ hrs.; Lac d'Oô – Refuge d'Espingo 1½ hrs.; return 2¼ hrs.; total time 5 hrs.
Difference in height: 828m.
Grade: easy walk on old roadway as far as Lac d'Oô; good walking path with sections of steep ascent up to the Refuge d'Espingo. On GR10 all the way.
Refreshments: Granges d'Astau; Refuge Lac d'Oô; Refuge d'Espingo.
Refuge: Refuge Lac d'Oô (1.05.-15.10.); B: 24; ℂ 05.61.79.12.29; Refuge d'Espingo (1.5.-15.10.); B: 80; ℂ 05.61.79.20.01.

The prettily embedded Lac d'Oô and the spectacle of the high waterfall at the end of the lake attract hoards of hikers in the summer to its shores. Far fewer of them continue up the path to the Refuge d'Espingo, picturesquely situated at the edge of the mountain basin of the same name. Two beautiful lakes on the high green plateau make an appealing contrast to the high mountain landscape all around.
The sign-posted path to Lac d'Oô begins along the road near to les **Granges d'Astau**. This immediately becomes a broad roadway and crosses the stream. On a moderately ascending path you walk up the valley and on the steep slopes opposite you can look at the attractive shape of the Cascade Chevelure de la Madeleine.

Refuge d'Espingo above the lake of the same name.

As the path steadily but easily ascends, you walk through a forest affording you some shade. Then the steep ascending bends begin in earnest and only slacken off at the yellow sign to Lac d'Oô. Very soon the dam of the lake comes into view. If you want to make an intermediary stop at the refuge by the lake, cross over the outflowing stream at the old arched bridge below the dam and after a short ascent you reach the hut at **Lac d'Oô**, 1504m.

The GR to Refuge d'Espingo leads left past the dam and at first climbs diagonally, then round back-breaking bends up across the shore-side slopes. Ascending through forest, grassy slopes you quickly gain height above the lake, then the path levels out again and traverses the slope past two beautifully cascading and fast-flowing streams. Another series of persistently ascending bends begins. The rocky path is stepped in places and steadily leads across slopes with alpine roses up to the Col d'Espingo. You are then standing on the col at the threshold of a sunken plateau with Lacs Saussat and d'Espingo. Turn right and in a few minutes you are at the **Refuge d'Espingo**, 1950m, which sits enthroned above the lake of the same name. From here you have a good view of the mountain formations in the Cirque d'Espingo. Just before the refuge a path starts down into the hollow to the two lakes and then divides further below. The right-hand path goes to Lac d'Espingo and straight on continues across a green valley bottom to Lac Saussat.

37 Pic de Céc"iré, 2403m

On the Chemin des Crêtes to a marvellous viewpoint

Superbagnères – Pic de Cécire

Location: Bagnères-de-Luchon, 625m.
Starting point: Superbagnères car park, 1804m. Approach from Bagnères-de-Luchon on the D125 and D46 into the Vallée du Lis and up to the Superbagnères ski station.
Walking times: Superbagnères – Pic de Cécire 2 hrs.; return 1¾ hrs; total time 3¾ hrs.
Difference in height: 599m.

Grade: easy walk with some short sections of quite steep ascent; well-laid GR10 path. The Chemin des Crêtes runs partly across long steep slopes (not recommended for those who suffer from vertigo).
Refreshments: Bagnères-de-Luchon.
Tip: there's also a cable car to Superbagnères from the village in the valley of Bagnères-de-Luchon.

Amongst the pre-summits of Luchon central massif, Pic de Cécire stands in a class of its own with its wide-angled lens perspective. There's a vast array of famous peaks between the Besiberri massif in the east and the Néouvielle peaks in the west. The Chemin des Crêtes high above Vallée du Lis is a brilliant panoramic path.

At **Superbagnères** car park you start the walk along a track going southwards. It immediately turns to the west (there's an information board here on a small projection close to the path). Go past lift stations and at the junction take the left-hand fork to Pic Ceciré according the signpost. The track directly becomes a roadway and the actual Chemin des Crêtes begins at a *cabane* on the right of the path.

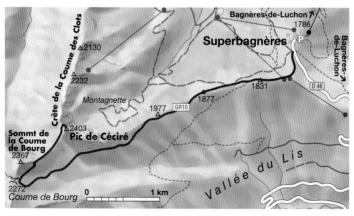

One of the numerous views from Pic de Cécíré: Cirque de Crabioules.

Always keeping below the line of the ridge and with varying gradients the path climbs up the very steep slopes of the crest which rises up to Pic de Cécíré at the end.

On the other side of the Vallée du Lis is the enormous Cirque de Crabioules with its glaciers and elegantly proportioned 3000ers. The path over the crest eventually enters a hilly valley coming down from the Col de la Coum de Bourg. Continue ascending towards the col, but turn off right from the GR before it at a waymarked fork (Ceciré is written in white on rock) to climb up across the slope in a north-easterly direction. At a prominent fork in the path take the steeper branch, then change immediately onto the other slope of the crest where the summit section of Ceciré begins. Cross the western slope towards the edge of the steep precipices and turn south-eastwards there to climb the last few metres along the ridge up to **Pic de Ceciré**, 2403m.

38 Short round walk in Vallée du Lis

Forests, gorges and thundering waterfalls

Auberge du Lis – Prairie de l'Artigue – Gouffre d'Enfer – Cascade d'Enfer – Auberge du Lis

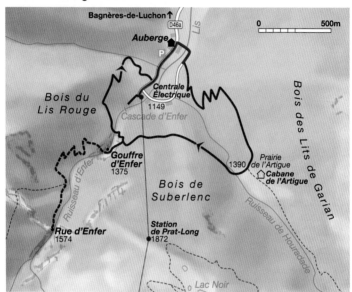

Location: Bagnères-de-Luchon, 625m.
Starting point: car park at the end of the road into Vallée du Lis, 1132m. Approach from Bagnères-de-Luchon on the D125 and D46 into Vallée du Lis. At the turn-off to Superbagnères continue along the valley road D46a.
Walking times: Auberge du Lis – Prairie de l'Artigue ¾ hr.; Prairie de l'Artigue – Gouffre d'Enfer ½ hr.; Gouffre d'Enfer – Cascade d'Enfer ¾ hr; Cascade d'Enfer – Auberge du Lis ¼ hr.; total time 2¼ hrs.
Difference in height: 260m.
Grade: easy round walk on marked hiking paths. Continuously steep incline to the

Prairie de l'Artigue. The sections of path are marked with the numbers 40, 42 and 43.
Refreshments: Auberge du Lis.
Alternative: Rue d'Enfer, 1574m. Impressive rock ravine of the R^{au} d'Enfer. At the fork in the path to the Gouffre d'Enfer continue straight ahead to the stone bridge where you change over onto the other side of the stream.
The path climbs up the steep wooded slope and then comes to a streambed which you follow uphill as far as the start of the gorge. 2 hrs there and back from the Gouffre d'Enfer.

Three thousand metre high rock bastions of the Cirque des Crabioules close off the green valley of the Lis. The water from the whole of this basin collects in the R^{au} d'Enfer, which does credit to its name. The 'stream of hell' has, in many places, cut a deep and narrow bed for itself in the rock and created impressive gorges and waterfalls which you can see close at hand on this easy round walk through beautiful forests.

Just before the **Auberge du Lis** cross the bridge over the valley stream and continue along the road until you come to the hiking path turning off left with signposts. The path directly enters the forest, zigzags unrelentingly up the steep slope of the R^{au} de Houradade and then runs more on the level above the stream through beech trees and pines. A bend to the south-west brings you to the edge of the grass-covered **Prairie de l'Artigue**, 1390m, where the path divides.

Thundering waterfalls of the Cascade d'Enfer.

Lac Vert (see Walk 39) and the Refuge Maupas (see Walk 40) are sign-posted left, but you keep straight ahead to the Gouffre d'Enfer. After the little bridge over a small stream gorge you go gently up and down through a pretty wood overgrown with moss. After a while the path crosses a water pipe and a cable car track, then descends before quickly winding down to some crossroads. Go left here to two viewing balconies with walls around them (sign 'promontoire') at the **Gouffre d'Enfer**, 1375m. The second lower balcony in particular gives you a stunning view of the dramatically narrow and steep gorge. Back at the fork, the path now quickly winds down to a bridge and over to the other side of the R^{au} d'Enfer. There's another short ascent here, then you follow the leisurely bends through the forest down the valley as far as the electricity works. Take the road to the right and continue along the path to the gloomy exit of the gorge from where the great mass of water thunders down from the **Cascade d'Enfer**, 1159m. The road leads back to the car park at the **Auberge du Lis**.

39 Lac Vert, 2001m

A lake in a picturesque setting with a 3000er as a backdrop

Auberge du Lis – Prairie de l'Artigue – Cabane de la Coume – Lac Vert and back

Location: Bagnères-de-Luchon, 625m.
Starting point: car park at the end of the road into the Vallée du Lis, 1132m. Approach from Bagnères-de-Luchon on the D125 and D46 into the Vallée du Lis, at the turn-off to Superbagnères continue along the valley road D46a.
Walking times: Auberge du Lis – Prairie de l'Artigue ¾ hr.; Prairie de l'Artigue – C^{ne} de la Coume 1hr.; C^{ne} de la Coume – Lac Vert 1¼ hrs; return 2½ hrs.; total time 5½ hrs.
Difference in height: 869m.
Grade: long walk with some sections of steep gradient. The sections of the path are marked with the number 40.
Refreshments: Auberge du Lis.
Alternative: an alternative return along the Refuge-du-Maupas route. Cross the outflow of the stream along the north side of the lake, continue across the slope on an almost horizontal path, at times at the edge of steep slopes. Then the path descends gradually and meets the path to the Refuge du Maupas above the small Lac Noir. Descend here to the right as in Walk No. 40.

The scenically diverse walk to Lac Vert leads through the long valley of the R^{au} de Houradade. The prettily embedded lake lies in a green basin on the hillside above the valley and is dominated in the south by the majestic Pic de Maupas and its neighbouring peaks.

For the first section of the route you follow Walk No. 38 and turn off left at the **Prairie de l'Artigue**, 1390m. This path leads along past the C^{ne} de l'Artigue which is on your left, runs through the pretty meadows and enters a thin forest. You now ascend a steeper path again above the R^{au} de Houradade and pass two streams in a gorge which plunge down to the valley stream on the opposite side; the second C^{de} de Houradade is especially beautiful. Soon afterwards you arrive at a second fork where the path going off right continues to the Refuge Maupas.

Lac Vert fills up a small hollow in a steep hillside.

Ascend straight on past this up to the higher valley with the **Cabane de la Coume**, 1715m, keeping close to the stream with the Col de Pinata in your sights.

At the foot of the col the path divides again with a series of bends climbing up the hillside left to the col and the winding path to the right leading to Lac Vert. Take the path to the right as it zigzags quickly up the slope to a hollow in the hillside with the tiny Lac des Grauès. After you have crossed the inflow of the lake, the path swings westwards and heads up towards a small col where you descend on the other side to the shore of the horseshoe-shaped **Lac Vert**, 2001m.

40 Long walk around the lakes via the Refuge du Maupas, 2430m

A superb, long and strenuous walk in the midst of the most beautiful mountain and lakeland scenery

Auberge du Lis – Refuge du Maupas – Lac Bleu – Lac Charles – Lac Célinda – Col de Pinata – Auberge du Lis

Location: Bagnères-de-Luchon, 625m.
Starting point: car park at the end of the road into the Vallée du Lis, 1132m. Approach from Bagnères-de-Luchon on the D125 and D46 into the Vallée du Lis. At the turn-off to Superbagnères continue along the valley road D46a.
Walking times: Auberge du Lis – Refuge du Maupas 3¾ hrs.; Refuge du Maupas – Lac Bleu ¾ hr.; Lac Bleu – Lac Charles ½ hr.; Lac Charles – Lac Célinda ½ hr.; Lac Célinda – Col de Pinata ¾ hr.; Col de

Pinata – Auberge du Lis 2 hrs.; total time 8¼ hrs.
Difference in height: 1298m.
Grade: very long and strenuous round walk with a big variation in height, but good paths. There are some hard and steep sections of ascent and for a short way the descent to the col is very steep.
Refreshments: Auberge du Lis; Refuge du Maupas.
Refuge: Refuge du Maupas (15.06.- 15.09.); B: 35; ✆ 05.61.79.16.07.

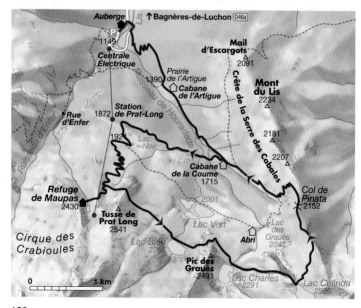

Several high mountain basins lie along the route.

Diversity and contrasts in the landscape characterize this brilliant walk which brings you close to the huge mountain ranges, glacier basins and cirque lakes. The Refuge de Maupas, first stopping-off point on the steep climb out of the valley, lies at the edge of the large Cirque de Crabioules. From there a fantastic high mountain path sets off along beside the three lakes which persist in their hollows in the cirque at the foot of the glaciated slopes of Pic de Maupas and its eastern neighbouring peak. The exciting descent along the ridge to the Col de Pinata and through the delightful valley of the Rᵃᵘ de Houradade is a perfect conclusion to a fabulous day's walk. For the first part of the route you follow Walk No. 39 as far as the fork beyond the Cᵈᵉ de Houradade. Continue right here and immediately cross the stream and with a sharp change in direction the path now turns to the west and for a long way you keep through meadows of flowers and single birch trees. After you have crossed two more little streams in quick succession you walk through meadows beside a rippling valley stream which cuts across a thinly wooded hilltop further on.

The path goes round the cleft with a steep incline on the right-hand slope of

Refuge de Maupas in front of the Cirque de Crabioules.

the hilltop and comes out onto a sloping terrace called Prat-Long at the end of which you can see the intermediary station of the electricity works cable car. Head towards it at first, walk past the Cⁿᵉ de Prat-Long with its round roof and turn to the south before the station.

A rapid ascent up the slope brings you above the small Lac Noir, then a connecting path leads off left to Lac Vert while your path goes directly towards the pipes and cable car track and goes into a long series of steeply winding bends uphill. You reach the fork to Lac Bleu along the stony path and this is where you turn off to the Refuge du Maupas. Following the sign for the refuge you zigzag further up the slope as far as a supporting pillar with an inscription in red which says 'Refuge CAF Maupas'. Cross below the pipes and follow the now level path across the other hillside over to the **Refuge du Maupas**, 2430m. (If you miss this spot, keep zigzagging up on the left of the pipes which disappear further up in the mountain. Just beforehand there's an opportunity to cross over below them and an obvious path then leads you to the refuge.)

From the refuge you descend at first back to the junction and take the path branching off right which is waymarked in blue. It heads towards the first slope of the Tusse du Prat Long, crosses it and then runs horizontally along the precipitous slopes. On the right above you can see the remaining glaciers of the Pic du Maupas. Lac Vert glistens on the left below and the pointed Pics de Sacroux and d'Estauas lie ahead. The first of the lakes comes into sight quickly and the path leads slightly downhill and is secured with a handrail along a steeply sloping section of the path and reaches **Lac Bleu** dam, 2265m. Go across the dam to the other side where a path descends to Lac Vert. Stay on the path going straight ahead, head towards the north flank of Pic de Grauès across stony ground and zigzag steeply up the rock. (A slightly exposed spot is made secure with a cable.) The path then continues up a comfortable incline and runs across the steep slope over to a rock spur, beyond which you turn into the next cirque valley. Lac Charles, also with a dam, emerges after a short crossing of a scree slope and its steep back walls provide a dramatic backdrop. Once you have arrived at the almost circular **Lac Charles**, 2291m, cross over the small dam and follow the path turning eastwards which gently ascends. After you have walked across a steeply sloping grassy hillside the path becomes a track straightened with large boulders which cover over a water pipe. It ends at **Lac Célinda**, 2395m, where you cross the outflow stream. Immediately afterwards at a cairn the path swivels distinctly to the north-east and continues across gently undulating terrain. It maintains height at first, is very distinct and is guided by cairns through the boulders, then descends towards the crest which swings to the north-west between the Pics de Sacroux and d'Estauas. Looking back you can see the glacial cirques of the summit face near Pic de Maupas and Lac Vert again on the terrace on the slope below left.

The path now runs over the gently grassy ridge of the crest which drops away steeply to the right while you enjoy wonderful views over into the Spanish valley of Val d'Aran. The crest gradually drops away, the path gets more precipitous and from time to time very steep. It swings briefly to the west and descends narrow zigzags down the slope. Running in a northerly direction towards the narrow ridge of the col, it then goes round a rock tower to the right and immediately afterwards arrives at the **Col de Pinata**, 2152m. Go left there and directly across the slope of the col, then round bends quickly down into the valley where you meet the path to Lac Vert. Now go down the valley along the stream to the C^{ne} de la Coume where, shortly afterwards, you meet the ascent path and descend to the **Auberge du Lis**.

41 Cirque de la Glère, 1559m

Peaceful round walk through a pretty circle of mountains

Vallée de la Pique – Cirque de la Glère – Hospice de France – Vallée de la Pique

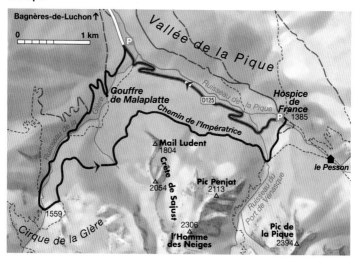

Location: Bagnères-de-Luchon, 625m.
Starting point: D125, about 3km beyond the turn-off from the D46 into Vallée du Lis, 1020m; take the forest path branching off to the right from the road sign-posted to the Cirque de la Glère. You can park at the side of the road.
Walking times: starting point – Cirque de la Glère 1¾ hrs.; Cirque de la Glère – Hospice de France 1¼ hrs.; Hospice de France – starting point ¾ hr.; total time 3¾ hrs.

Difference in height: 539m.
Grade: some sections of steep climbing on the path to the Cirque de la Glère, from there an effortless stroll along the Chemin de l'Impératrice to the Hospice de France. About a 4km return along the road.
Refreshments: Bagnères-de-Luchon.
Tip: this round walk can also be done in the opposite direction.
Either way you can hitch-hike along the road to save yourself the walk there and back.

The rather modestly sized Cirque de la Glère is not without its own charm. The beautifully formed mountains, waterfalls, steep green hillsides and pretty valley meadows of the mountain basin together form a delightful landscape which can be explored on this varied round walk.
Start the walk along the **roadway** and go as far as a narrow right-hand bend

where a path branches off and takes you to a bridge over a streambed. Just afterwards past a bridge on the left and a small dam, climb up the slope on the right and meet a roadway which you follow to the left.

After a few minutes you arrive at the Gouffre de Malaplatte, an impressive narrowing of the gorge of the R^{au} de la Glère. Continue along the roadway which winds uphill to a sharp right-hand bend where a yellow arrow (No. 31/34) indicates the hiking path going straight ahead. Leave the roadway here and go up the valley above a stream through woods. The narrowing path gets nearer to the stream again and comes to a *passerelle* (footbridge) where you change over onto the other side. Just after that you come to a fork.

Following the yellow waymarkers you now climb up the steep path as it winds its way up the wooded

Cirque de la Glère.

slope until the path becomes noticeably flatter and leads you across a second *passerelle* to the other side of the stream again. It now stays beside the stream and runs through the pretty hollow to the extensive valley floor of the **Cirque de la Glère**, 1559m.

The valley path divides here; to the right it goes up to the Col de Sacroux and Port de la Glère, to the left across the stream and then on a bend to the east it joins the Chemin de l'Impératrice. Now walk down the valley along the comfortable hiking path through a shady wood. It slowly curves to the east, leads out of a wooded 'gorge' and swings finally into the Vallée de la Pique.

Walk through the splendid beech wood from where you are afforded many beautiful views of the green mountain ranges in the east that form the border with Val d'Aran. At Pont de Penjat you come to the path over the pass to Port de Benasque. Go left and cross the stream, then continue along the roadway to the old buildings of the **Hospice de France**, 1385m. A few metres along to the left bring you to the car park where the walk back on the road to your starting point begins.

42 Refuge de Benasque, 2248m, and Port de Benasque, 2444m

Classic route onto a pass with magnificent views

Hospice de France – Refuge de Benasque – Port de Benasque and back

Location: Bagnères-de-Luchon, 625m.
Starting point: Hospice de France (car park), 1385m.
Approach from Luchon on the D125 to the end of the road.
Walking times: Hospice de France – Refuge de Benasque 2½ hrs.; Refuge de Benasque – Port de Benasque ½ hr.; return 2½ hrs.; total time 5½ hrs.
Ascent: 1059m.
Grade: moderate walk on well-laid path up to the pass, yellow waymarkers; many sections of steep climbing.
Refreshments: Bagnères-de-Luchon; Refuge de Benasque.
Refuge: Refuge de Benasque (1.06.-30.09); B: 12; ✆ 05.61.79.26.46.

The ascent to the pass over into the Spanish Benasque valley leads past the Refuge de Benasque that lies by several deep cirque lakes at the foot of the sheer Pics de Sauvegarde and de la Mine. From there it's only a half hour ascent to the cleft of Port de Benasque that provides you with a view of the Maladeta massif with the highest peaks of the Pyrenees. The impressive mountain scenery with the glistening glaciers stands in striking contrast to the high green pastures through which the Río Ésera meanders. One of the most beautiful Pyrenean walks!

At the **Hospice de France** (the inn, which is full of tradition, is unfortunately derelict, but is supposed to be renovated in 2003) follow the signpost for Port de Benasque. After the bridge over the stream the path begins slowly to ascend. Go past the turn-off left to the Étangs de la Frèche and cross the stream over a bridge. The Chemin de l'Impératrice turns off right (see Walk 41), but you keep straight on and climb up the valley hillside. The path now continues up round wide bends on which you steadily gain height. Round one bend after another it ascends across hillsides covered in grass and flowers up to a small valley basin where the waterfalls, which have already been in sight for a while, join together to form a stream. A path goes straight on here to the waterfalls, but you follow the yellow waymarkers and cross the R^{au} du Port de Benasque. Immediately after that the path zigzags again uphill and is interrupted further up by a flat section where you cross over a side-stream and head towards the valley stream. Just beforehand, the path swings up the steep slope again and winds its way uphill. You pass by a dilapidated shelter on a ledge and then climb the hill beyond where the small **Refuge de Benasque**, 2248m, lies hidden at the edge of Boums du Port, situated in a picturesque location.

To ascend the pass, keep on the path along the shore of the lake. (An alternative path climbs up the hillside directly by the refuge and meets the path again further up). It leads to the biggest of the four lakes and then starts up a steep incline. The way over the pass still lies hidden behind the jagged rock bastion of Pic de la Minet and not until you have zigzagged up the steep slope to the col is the rock arch visible above. Another last few rapid bends and you are standing on **Port de Benasque**, 2444m. The green valley plain of the Río Ésera stretches out below whilst the massive glacier of the Maladeta rises up opposite with Pico de Aneto, at 3404m, the highest peak in the Pyrenees.

Port de Benasque: opposite Pico de Aneto and Maladeta.

43 Long walk in the mountains around the Hospice de France

Magnificent scenery

Hospice de France – Port de Benasque – Port dera Picada – Pas de la Mounjoye – Hospice de France

Location: Bagnères-de-Luchon, 625m.
Starting point: Hospice de France (car park), 1385m. Approach from Luchon on the D125 to the end of the road.
Walking times: Hospice de France – Port de Benasque 3 hrs.; Port de Benasque – Port de la Picada 1 hr.; Port de la Picada – Pas de Mounjoye 1 hr.; Pas de Mounjoye – Hospice de France 1 hr. ; total time 6 hours.

Difference in height: 1200m (with some ascents in between).
Grade: walk with a big height variation, demanding fitness; path waymarked in yellow. Some steep gradients on the ascent to Port de Benasque.
Refreshments: Bagnères-de-Luchon; Refuge de Benasque.
Refuge: Refuge de Benasque (1.06.- 30.09); B: 12; ✆ 05.61.79.26.46.

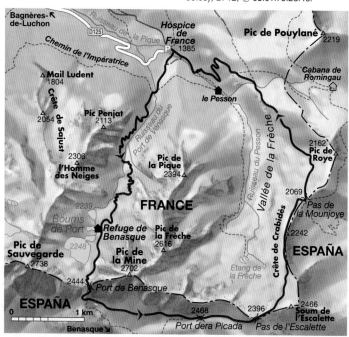

View of Val d'Aran from Port de las Picada.

Dark blue mountain lakes, wonderfully luxuriant meadows covered with flowers, high green pastures, sheer rocky peaks and large expanses of glacier – no landscape could be more varied! This round path over three mountain passes in the region bordering with Spain is bursting with beautiful and thrilling images and gives you a fascinating insight into the mountain scenery on both sides.

From the **Hospice de France** follow Walk 42 as far as **Port de Benasque**, 2444m. First descend the slope round bends to a green waymarked turn-off right which you walk past. A few steps further on, you turn off left from the dirt path going straight ahead onto a relatively broad grassy path that quickly becomes a well-trodden narrower path. On a gentle incline it runs eastwards with views of the high green plateau of the Plan de Aiguallut at the foot of Pico de Aneto. After a large funnel-shape caused by falling scree the path slowly ascends and runs across a scree slope.

Precipitous spikes form the French-Spanish border.

On the right below lie several pools. Now begins the start of the climb up the slope to the col. You can easily make out the path on the right-hand side which comes up from La Besurta plateau. The path heads for the top of the broad col in a straight line across the slope and finally winds steeply uphill to reach **Port dera Picada**, 2468m. In the gently undulating hollows of the slope ahead lie several tiny pools, enclosed on the right-hand side by steep rocky flanks. Follow the mule track across the slope on the left down to the Pas de l'Escalette and at the sign-posted fork turn off left in the direction of Cloth de Lunfèrn.

The path now climbs along the jagged ridge, then changes onto the other side and begins to descend. Go past a trig point, then a stone tower and now follow the Crête de Crabidès that drops abruptly down into Val d'Aran. The beautiful mountain path offers magnificent views steeply down into the Vallée de la Frèche on the left below and over to the dramatically shaped Crête de la Pique with its pointed Pic de la Pique.

The v-shaped cleft on the right marks the Port de Benasque.

After the last spikes of the mountain chain – on the left below in the valley you can see the Hospice de France – the path strikes out to the right and arrives at the **Pas de la Mounjoye**, 2069m, with a junction and signposts. It is possible to descend from here into Val d'Aran, but you go in a northerly direction again and walk quickly downhill straight across grassy hillsides. Past a cattle fence you walk high above the valley through increasingly colourful meadows of flowers to a crossroads. Ignore the path on the right to the Cne de Roumingau and follow the signpost for Hospice de France par Fontaine Rouge, turning off left. A little later you come through some fencing and then to the enclosed Fontaine Rouge at the side of the path on the right in the midst of a sea of flowers.

Go downhill round some easy-angled bends through wonderful beech woods to the valley stream and from there walk back to the **Hospice de France**.

44 Pic de Bacanère, 2193m

Pretty meadowed slopes and a fabulous panorama

Artigue – Cabane de Saunères – Col de Peyrehitte – Pic de Bacanère and back

Location: Juzet-de-Luchon, 625m.
Starting point: Artigue (car park), 1224m. Approach from Luchon on the D27 to Juzet-de-Luchon, there take the D46 to Sode and Artigue; car park before the village.
Walking times: Artigue – Cabane de Saunères 1 hr.; Cabane de Saunères – Col de Peyrehitte 1 hr.; Col de Peyrehitte –

Pic de Bacanère 1 hr.; return 2½ hrs.; total time: 5½ hrs.
Difference in height: 969m.
Grade: an easy walk to the Cne de Saunères on a roadway (GR10); long walk to Pic de Bacanère, but without any technical difficulties (GR10 alternative).
Refreshments: Juzet-de-Luchon; Artigue (restaurant only).

In itself, the pretty village of Artigue is not without brilliant views of the mountains around Luchon, but even more so is the GR10 to Pic de Bacanère, where the breathtaking view into the distance improves with every step and culminates on the easy summit in a 360° panorama. 'Bacanère' means 'vache noire' (black cow) and the name reminds you that the hillsides around Pic de Bacanère were once a rich pasture area.

Go through Artigue as far as the church at the northern end of the village where the sign-posted GR ascends the road and leaves it after 50m along a roadway.

Intermediary stop: Cabane de Saunères.

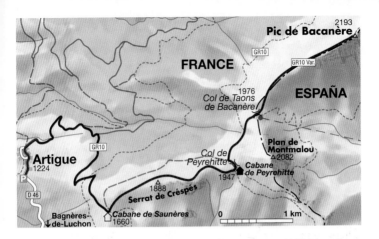

This winds up a steeper incline across the flower-covered hillsides above Artigue. After a short stretch through the woods it temporarily splits into two – the fork to the right is less strenuous – and comes together again before the Forêt Domaniale d'Artigue. Now walk through the mixed forest and afterwards across the slopes covered in heather. Ignore the sign-posted path to the C^ne de Salode on the left and the following wide bend of the roadway brings you to the **Cabane de Saunères**, 1660m, a small and pleasant shepherds' hut (room for several people) in a wonderful position.

Do not continue along the track, but take instead the white and red marked path behind the *cabane* which ascends north-eastwards up the grassy slope. As you reach further up you walk through a pretty landscape of ridges towards a prominent hilltop, go round it to the left and then climb up again onto the more level crest of the ridge where the view opens up of the mountain ranges in the south.

Continuing eastwards you meet a dew-pond (with a sign to a spring which is a five minute walk away along the GR) and the **Col de Peyrehitte**, 1947m, beyond which the *cabane* of the same name lies hidden. Instead of following the descending GR path along the grassy track, take the path across the slope that goes off by the pond and runs at the same height across the slopes of Montmajou overgrown with heather. Further along this you meet the GR alternative (it turns off from the track at a solar panel) and climb up right to the Col des Taons de Bacanère with the remains of a transport cable car. From the col ascend gently uphill at first to the right along the crest of the slope then along the elongated ridge beside waymarkers as far as **Pic de Bacanère**, 2193m.

45 Refuge des Estagnous, 2245m

Into the centre of the Mont Valier national park

Pla de la Lau – Cascade de Nérech – Refuge des Caoussis – Refuge des Estagnous and back

View from the refuge.

Location: Castillon-en-Couserans, 520m.
Starting point: Pla de la Lau (car park), 930m.
Approach from Castillon-en-Couserans on the D4 in the direction of Sentein, turning off left via Ayer into Vallée du Ribérot as far as the car park.
Walking times: Pla de la Lau – Cascade de Nérech 1¾ hrs.; Cascade de Nérech – Refuge des Caoussis 1¼ hrs.; Refuge des Caoussis – Refuge des Estagnous 1¼ hrs.; return 3½ hrs.; total time 7¾ hrs.
Difference in height: 1315m.
Grade: effortless walk as far as the C^de^ de Nèrech; demanding ascent with big height variation to the Refuge des Estagnous.
Well-laid paths, red and white waymarkers.
Refreshments: Castillon-en-Couserans; Refuge des Estagnous.
Refuge: Refuge des Estagnous (1.06.-30.09.); B: 70; ℂ 05.61.96.76.22.
Alternative: Etang Rond, 1929m. At the sign-posted fork turn right after the Refuge des Caoussis. The path crosses the stream which comes down from the Estagnous lakes and eventually reaches the Etang Rond. 1 hr., there and back from the fork.

This gentle ascent through the long valley of the R^au^ de Ribérot as far as the impressive C^de^ de Nérech is part of the Chemin du Valier that opens up the inner nature reserve. The mountains around the Mont Valier massif are displayed at their best up along the path to the Refuge des Estagnous. The hut is located on a magnificent viewing platform in the shadow of the towering Mont Valier.

At the **Pla de la Lau** car park cross the bridge over the side-stream and follow the sign-posted hiking path on the right of the valley stream. Past the bridge over which the GR10 turns off left at the following fork, with Cap des

Lauses and Le Muscadet sign-posted left, and keep going straight on. A little later the path changes over onto the other side of the stream on two small bridges and continues alongside it up the valley.

The path begins to ascend as it enters a beech wood, then runs again across the flat and open valley floor and comes to another bridge on which you cross the valley stream. The striking cascade and the summit sections of Mont Valier have in the meantime come into view. Always keeping close to the stream, the path runs through a beautiful beech wood and reaches the base of the **Cascade de Nérech**, 1350m, which guides and bundles the crashing water through a jutting slab of rock.

The climb to the Refuge des Estagnous (sign for Mont Valier) continues over the bridge at the foot of the cascade. The path skilfully makes its way round the steep head of the valley by going left up the slope and after a strenuous incline reaches a small platform. The valley hillside opposite is cut off by a beautifully textured rock wall over which fall numerous tumbling cascades. First walk through the luxuriantly green valley towards the broad cascade of the R^{au} de Ribérot, but then turn off left and climb the precipitous slopes round bends. After this section the path becomes noticeably flatter and arrives at the unstaffed **Refuge des Caoussis**, 1859m.

Immediately after the hut the path divides. Right goes to the Etang Rond, amongst other places, (see alternative), but you continue straight ahead and cross the slopes which become markedly steeper and are covered in granite boulders and rhododendron bushes. The view of the beautifully framed Etang Rond improves with increasing height and further on the hut also becomes visible above a ledge in the slope. The path finally gets steep, goes round a few bends and arrives at the **Refuge des Estagnous**, 2245m, where your exertions are rewarded with fantastic views. The tiny Estagnous lakes lie to the south of the hut while in the east you can see the towering summit of Mont Valier.

46 Long round walk in the Mont Valier national park

Demanding day's walk with spectacular scenery

Pla de la Lau – Refuge des Estagnous – Col de Pécouch – Cap des Lauses – Pla de la Lau

Location: Castillon-en-Couserans, 520m.
Starting point: Pla de la Lau (car park), 930m. Approach from Castillon-en-Couserans on the D4 in the direction of Sentein, turning left via Ayer into the Vallée du Ribérot as far as the car park.
Walking times: Pla de la Lau – Refuge des Estagnous 4¼ hrs.; Refuge des Estagnous – Col de Pécouch ¾ hr.; Col de Pécouch – Cap des Lauses 2¼ hrs.; Cap des Lauses – Pla de la Lau 2¼ hrs., total time 9½ hrs.
Difference in height: 1600m (with some ascents in between).
Grade: altogether a very strenuous walk with a big height variation; at times over rough terrain. Red and white waymarkers as far as the Refuge des Estagnous, yellow waymarkers up to the Cap des Lauses; then GR path. Dangerous descent in the mist!
Refreshments: Castillon-en-Couserans; Refuge des Estagnous.
Refuge: Refuge des Estagnous (1.06.-30.09.); B: 70; ✆ 05.61.96.76.22.

The climb up to the Refuge des Estagnous can be extended into a wonderful round walk which leads you back through the R^au de Muscadet valley. The wealth of beautiful landscape images and sharp contrasts make this demanding walk not only very enjoyable, but also totally exhilarating. A brilliant walk in the heart of the Mont Valier massif!

The round walk begins with the ascent up to the **Refuge des Estagnous** as in Walk 45. After the hut there's a signpost for the Col de Pécouch. The yellow waymarked path is indicated to the north and winds its way up the steep incline of the grassy slope scattered with small granite humps. Just below the col it goes over steep rock where a bit of scrambling is necessary before reaching the **Col de Pécouch**, 2462m. The col forms a striking scenic contrast between the green R^au de Ribérot valley and the dramatic and bare granite slopes ahead, in between which patches of grass have established themselves. The strange terrain shows clear signs of intense glacial activity. The path is waymarked with cairns and yellow paint. First of all it goes to the left away from the col, keeps in a north-westerly direction, and runs quite clearly over the stony terrain with gentian and low bushes of alpine roses in between. Then the path sets off in a northerly direction and heads directly for the cleft ahead where the elongated valley basin encloses two pretty lakes. It now descends steeply down the grassy slope, at times crosses over boulders and comes to the north-western end of the Etang de Milouga, where you cross the outflow.

A few metres up the slope then the path turns down the valley and runs, constantly up and down, across the valley slope. Cross over

Finally through a secluded beech wood.

quite a few side-streams on the way, pass a spring which comes out of the rock and continue left at a junction (yellow waymarkers). At roughly the same height it leads to the C^{ne} de Tous. On the right past the shepherds' hut you go over a projection, then across the gentle grassy slope with fencing and continue beyond that to **Cap des Lauses**, 1892m.

At the fork you follow the GR path on the left of the slope to the col. It descends round easy-angled bends and goes beside the R^{au} d'Aouen, which emerges on the slope on the way, and approaches the C^{ne} d'Aouen. The shepherds' hut lies on your right a little away from the path that crosses the valley stream and continues to zigzag down the slope. Later on it touches a scree slope and winds through a beech wood. As soon as you get close to the R^{au} de Muscadet the path turns westwards and crosses the R^{au} d'Aouen. After that it winds again through a shady wood as far as a signpost which indicates the starting point at Pla de la Lau. Cairns indicate the way left to the stream, but you follow the white and red waymarkers which take you on the right-hand bank of the stream as far as the bridge where you cross over back to the car park.

47 Ridge walk into the Vallée du Biros

Enjoyable round walk along a high mountain path with wonderful views

Balacet – Pic de l'Arraing – Pic de Sérau – Col des Morères – Balacet

Location: Sentein, 731m.
Starting point: at the entrance to the village of Balacet, 925m. Approach from Castillon-en-Couserans on the D4 in the direction of Sentein, turn right after Lascoux on the D704 as far as Balacet, park at the entrance to the village.
Walking times: Balacet – Pic de l'Arraing 1¾ hrs.; Pic de l'Arraing – Pic de Sérau 1 hr.; Pic de Sérau – Col des Morères ¼ hr.; Col des

Morères – Balacet 2 hrs.; total time 5 hrs.
Difference in height: 795m.
Grade: moderate round walk on partly waymarked paths. The approach to the Col de l'Arraing and the return are part of the du Biros walk, red and yellow waymarkings.The climb up to the Pic de l'Arraing and along the crest are waymarked in yellow.
Refreshments: Sentein.

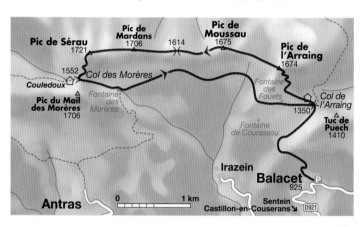

You can walk along the crest between Pics de l'Arraing and Sérau on a beautiful panoramic path which offers excellent views on all sides. Even from Pic de l'Arraing there are good views of the landscape of peaks between Pic de Maubermé and Mont Valier as well as over the valleys of Biros and Bellongue, so that you can shorten this round walk and just make a rewarding summit ascent.

The walk begins at the entrance to the village of **Balacet** at the signpost for Col de l'Arraing on the right of the road. The path goes up a steady incline through a shady wood. Where the path turns off to the right it changes direction to the west and continues straight ahead uphill through the forest, from time to time enclosed by dry stone walls. After the wood the path runs through an area of ferns to a level section of the slope. Keep going directly towards the col where a *cabane* immediately appears. At the **Col de l'Arraing**, 1350m, go across to the hut from which two paths set off to the west. The red and yellow marked path which runs horizontally across the slope, is the return path for this round walk, so for the ascent to Pic de L'Arraing, take the yellow waymarked path which climbs diagonally up the slope at first as a grassy track, then later as a more clearly trodden dirt path. The path then winds its way round long-drawn-out bends which bring you to **Pic de l'Arraing**, 1674m.

In the Vallée du Biros.

This round walk now continues along the crest. The path descends to the Pas de Moussau and then climbs up again to Pic de Moussau, 1675m, whose narrow ridge of the peak demands a bit of rock climbing. Immediately you descend again to the Col de Portet and from there along the long-drawn-out ridge up to Pic de Mardans, 1706m.

The last 'peak' of the crest is hardly pronounced and with a little bit of up and down you arrive at **Pic de Sérau**, 1721m. From there the path turns left at a waymarker on a block of stone. You can easily miss the point where the path continues because the waymarkers have been placed on flat stones on the grassy slope and the path is not very obvious at first. In a south-westerly direction you climb directly up towards your next destination, the Col de Morères. The ridge of the col with the Cⁿᵉ de Morères and a fenced-off field is always in sight so that you can easily descend the slope over rough terrain. At the **Col de Morères**, 1552 m, you come to a sign where you take the hiking path (waymarked yellow and red) leading left into a small crack in the slope. Ignore the path branching off horizontally left. The path comes directly past a large boulder with a waymarker and goes across the left-hand slope of the valley to a signpost where you follow the path left in the direction of Cap de l'Arraing. Past a hut on the left of the path you come to a wood which is thinned out in places later on due to the wind. Gently ascending at first, then mostly on the level, you walk below the crest back to the Col de l'Arraing.

Return to **Balacet** along the ascent path.

48 Port de Salau, 2087m

Onto the border pass into Val d'Aran

Salau – Cascade de Léziou – Cabane de Pouill – Port de Salau and back

Location: Salau, 850m.
Starting point: car park at the hiking path to the C^{de} de Léziou, 980m. Approach from Seix on the D3 via Couflens to Salau. At the southern end of the village continue for about another 1.2km along the road in the direction of the old mines; the sign-posted path turns off right at the hairpin bend going left.
Walking times: car park – C^{de} de Lèziou ½ hr.; C^{de} de Léziou – C^{ne} de Pouill 1¼ hrs.; C^{ne} de Pouill – Port de Salau 1½ hrs.; return 2¾ hrs.; 6 hrs. in total.
Difference in height: 1107m.
Grade: uncomplicated walk, but there's a large variation in height. Partly along an old mule path; the ascent to the col is very steep.
Yellow waymarkings.
Refreshments: Salau.

Port de Salau was previously an important pass for the transporting of wood which was cut on the Spanish side and taken over into France. Today this spacious border col is a beautiful viewpoint from where you can see the highest peaks of Val d'Aran at their best.

From the **car park** it's a leisurely walk along the roadway up the valley. First of all cross a side-stream and then the valley stream on little concrete bridges, and you come to the **Cascade de Léziou**, 1060m, which is hidden behind some trees on the left of the path. A signpost indicates the short detour to this secluded spot. Continue along the roadway that now quickly winds its way up the wooded slopes to a sign-posted junction near to the stream.

From here turn down right to the stream and on the other side after a short ascent you enter a forest. The shady path now heads down the valley for a while and then makes a sharp turn. Walk through the Bois de Lanette, past a turn-off right and the wood thins out and you come to an open grassy hillside. Cross two side-streams one after the other and afterwards the path temporarily becomes a rather indistinct grassy track which winds up the slope. On the now more obvious path again you pass by **Cabane de Pouill**, 1541m, which lies on the other side of the stream.

Heading towards an old cable car structure you go past a little water house and just before a stream, you reach a fork where you keep to the same side of the hillside and continue uphill round bends. When you come to another fork, go right along the broad grassy ledge and up the valley on a more level path heading towards two cable car pillars. Ignore a path branching off sharply to the right and come to a hut with a round roof where you take the moderately inclined path to the right. This then becomes a series of at first short, then lengthier zigzags, which climb up to the col. Once you have arrived on the broad ridge of the pass it's only another few steps over to **Port de Salau**, 2087m.

Beyond the mountains lies Val d'Aran.

49 Long round walk through the Cirque de Cagateille

Through the upper stages of a marvellous mountain basin

La Peyre – Passerelle de Cagateille – Etang de la Hillette – Etang d'Alet – La Peyre

Location: St. Lizier, 720m.
Starting point: La Peyre, car park at the end of the road to the Cirque de Cagateille, 1020m. Approach from Aulus-les-Bains on the D8 in the direction of Seix. Just before Le Trein go left onto the D38 in the direction of Cirque de Cagateille.
Walking times: La Peyre – Passerelle de Cagateille ¾ hr.; Passerelle de Cagateille – Etang de la Hillette 1¾ hrs.; Etang de la Hillette – Etang d'Alet 1½ hrs.; Etang d'Alet – La Peyre 2½ hrs.; total time 6½ hrs.
Difference in height: 1040m (with ascents in between).

Grade: the long round walk demands a good standard of fitness; sections of very steep ascent to the Etang de la Hillette; short passages of scrambling, secured in places. Yellow waymarkings.
Refreshments: St. Lizier.
Tip: the bridge over the R^{au} des Cors at the end of the round walk was destroyed in the summer of 2002. However you can cross the river under normal conditions about 10m downstream from the old bridge. From the car park it's 5 minutes to the river if you need to check on the level of the water.

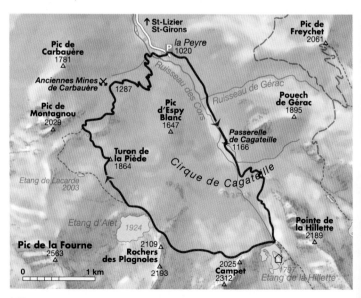

Etang d'Alet.

The Cirque de Cagateille is the most beautiful mountain valley of the Couserans, which ranks just behind the Cirque de Gavarnie. The wide amphitheatre consists of steep wooded slopes above which there's a wonderful towering circle of rock of limestone and granite. In the landscape sculpted by glaciers from the quaternary there are innumerable hollows where pretty lakes shimmer a beautiful blue and turquoise. The classic walk beyond to the head of the valley and the last waterfall can take up to a whole day and give you a fascinating insight into every facet of this glacial scenery.

At **La Peyre** car park the hiking path is sign-posted for Cagateille and La Hillette. After only a short ascent up the slope you can see the valley basin with the steep waterfalls. Walk up the valley through beech woods offering you some shade. On the way a sign indicates a little concrete bridge situated five metres above the point where you cross over the R^{au} de Gérac. Go across another side-stream just afterwards, then leave the forest. You can see ahead the round valley of beautifully formed rock walls and peaks towering up and the dome-shaped Pointe de la Hillette stands out below. Walk across the flat valley floor to the **Passerelle de Cagateille**, 1166m, and continue along the path on the other side of the bridge. The path heads in a

southerly direction and soon begins its rapid ascent up the hillside. At the signpost for Etang de la Hillette/Port de Couillac it abruptly changes direction to the north-east, but soon turns back again while still going up the hefty slope. In between times you have to climb up steeper rock where there are some iron rungs and cement steps to help you. There's also a rope handrail for safety further up. After a flat section the path runs steeply up the slope again at another signpost and runs mostly across bare rock. Then follows a steep grassy slope strewn with stone slabs until you reach a section of rock that is protected with a handrail. The path divides near to the stream gully. Left goes to Port de Couillac, but you go right and climb round a drop in the slope with a bit of scrambling, also made safe, down to the stream where you climb over granite boulders up to the **Etang de la Hillette**, 1797m. The delightful mountain lake is surrounded by beautiful rock formations and a path along its left-hand shore leads to a *cabane*.

Your path now crosses the outflow stream, goes over granite humps and winds its way up the hillside. Past the onion-shaped end of the long rock wall (the Falaises de Campet) the path goes across the northern slope of the rock face where a lot of granite boulders have collected at the bottom. Take careful note of the yellow waymarkers and cairns as you cross the scree slopes since the route is not always obvious and lots of small paths lead off nowhere. Continuing westwards across grassy slopes covered in rhododendrons you come to a stream that you cross at the marked spot and now keep heading north-west, over some more scree slopes, towards the ridge lying ahead (the Rochers des Plagnoles). The path goes up a steep slope around the rock spur and at this moment you have reached the highest point of the walk. The Etang d'Alet suddenly emerges here below you as well. The path quickly winds downhill and briefly touches the **Etang d'Alet**, 1924m, before descending to the stream that flows from the lake in a pretty waterfall.

Cross over this and follow the moderately ascending path to a small flat area with a large cairn where the final descent begins. You quickly descend the slope past a dry pond and a little further on the path bends to the east before rapidly descending a broad aisle in the slope. The path goes across slopes with forests and meadows, six feet high ferns and finally round long zigzag bends through beech woods down into the valley until it eventually changes into a forest track that leads to the bridge over the stream and back to La Peyre car park.

In a most beautiful and remote location: Etang de la Hillette.

50 Cascade d'Ars, 1485m

To one of the most beautiful cascades in the Pyrenees

Aulus-les-Bains – Cascade d'Ars – high valley of the Ruissau d'Ars and back

Location: Aulus-les-Bains, 750m.
Starting point: car park at the start of the hiking path to the Cascade d'Ars, 790m. Approach from Aulus-les-Bains on the D8 in the direction of Col de Latrape; after the bridge in Aulus-les-Bains you can park along a roadway that branches off immediately left on the first hairpin bend.
Walking times: car park – base of the Cascade d'Ars 1¾ hrs.; base of the Cascade d'Ars – high valley of the Rᵃᵘ d'Ars ½ hr.; return 2 hrs.; total time 4¼ hrs.

Difference in height: 695m.
Grade: easy walk on a roadway and GR10; several sections of the path have very steep inclines. GR sections are waymarked white and red.
Refreshments: Aulus-les-Bains.
Alternative: ascent from Aulus-les-Bains on the GR10. At the eastern end of the village the GR10 turns off right from the D8, just after the Col d'Agnès sign, going in the direction of the sign-post to Prabis. It joins up with the roadway at the top.

One of the famous pioneers of the 19th century, the Englishman Henry Russell, described the Cascade d'Ars as the most beautiful waterfall in the Pyrenees. Today, the GR1 goes past this imposing spectacle of thundering water located amidst luxuriant vegetation and gives you an easy opportunity of visiting a natural phenomenon. Most walkers turn round at the waterfall without climbing up to the delightful high valley from where the peaceful Rᵃᵘ d'Ars cascades. Extending the walk by another ½ hour is definitely worthwhile.

At the **car park** follow the sign-posted roadway. With a moderate incline it runs through the forest and reaches a turn-off over into the Vallée de Fouillet. Keep straight ahead and immediately the GR10, coming up from Aulus-les-Bains, joins from the left and you walk beside the Rᵃᵘ d'Ars flowing through a

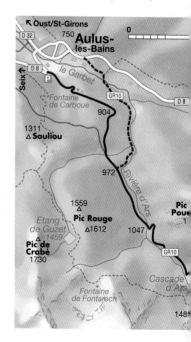

Cascade d'Ars: one of the most beautiful waterfalls in the Pyrenees.

pretty wooded ravine. The roadway becomes a hiking path and crosses the valley stream on the Pont de l'Artigou. With a few bends through a thin beech wood it's a constant steady uphill climb to where the waterfall begins. The path rises above the stream and then heads for the broad rocky ledge where the water spreads out after its steep drop. Past the fanned cascade the path winds on through the wood up to the huge **Cascade d'Ars**, 1350m, to which you can make a detour along a path to the right.

In order to climb above the waterfall the path swings round to the south-east onto the slope. From there it ascends some rapid bends and changes direction to the south-west. Going through a mixed forest of small bushes you come to the delightful **high valley of the Ruissau d'Ars**, 1485m, through which the stream gently meanders.

Index

abri	shelter	pont	bridge
barrage	dam	port	mountain pass
barrière	barrier	ravin	stream
bois	wood	refuge	refuge
cabane	(shepherd's) hut	rivière	river, stream
cascade	waterfall	ruisseau	torrent, stream
chemin	path	sentier	hiking path
cirque	mountain basin		(waymarked)
col	hill,	sommet	summit
	top of pass	source	spring, source
crête	crest, mountain	surgence	spring
	ridge	vallée	valley
étang	pond, lake		
falaise	rock face	**Regional Expressions**	
fontaine	spring, well	bat	small valley
gave	river	boum	lake
glacier	glacier	cap	peak
gorge	ravine,	clot	hollow, small
	gorge		basin
gouffre	ravine,	lis, lys	avalanche
	gorge	hount	spring
grange	barn	hourquette	pass, col
lac	lake	oule	cirque, basin
muraille	rock wall	pla	small plateau
passerelle	foot bridge	port	pass, col
pic	mountain peak	soum	rounded hilltop
piste	track, roadway	toue	shelter under a
plateau	high plain		rock
pointe	jagged spikes	tuc	peak

Abbreviations

GR (Grande Randonnée) long distance path (marked red and white)
HRP (Haute-Randonnée Pyrénéenne) Pyreneen high mountain hiking path
GRP (Grande Randonnée Pyrénéenne) Pyreneen long distance path
R^{au} = Ruisseau   stream
C^{de} = Cascade   waterfall
C^{ne} = Cabane   (shepherd's) hut